APARTMENT 3A

BY
JEFF DANIELS

DRAMATISTS
PLAY SERVICE
INC.

APARTMENT 3A
Copyright © 2000, Jeff Daniels

All Rights Reserved

CAUTION: Professionals and amateurs are hereby warned that performance of APARTMENT 3A is subject to payment of a royalty. It is fully protected under the copyright laws of the United States of America, and of all countries covered by the International Copyright Union (including the Dominion of Canada and the rest of the British Commonwealth), and of all countries covered by the Pan-American Copyright Convention, the Universal Copyright Convention, the Berne Convention, and of all countries with which the United States has reciprocal copyright relations. All rights, including professional/amateur stage rights, motion picture, recitation, lecturing, public reading, radio broadcasting, television, video or sound recording, all other forms of mechanical or electronic reproduction, such as CD-ROM, CD-I, DVD, information storage and retrieval systems and photocopying, and the rights of translation into foreign languages, are strictly reserved. Particular emphasis is placed upon the matter of readings, permission for which must be secured from the Author's agent in writing.

The English language stock and amateur stage performance rights in the United States, its territories, possessions and Canada for APARTMENT 3A are controlled exclusively by DRAMATISTS PLAY SERVICE, INC., 440 Park Avenue South, New York, NY 10016. No professional or nonprofessional performance of the Play may be given without obtaining in advance the written permission of DRAMATISTS PLAY SERVICE, INC., and paying the requisite fee.

Inquiries concerning all other rights should be addressed to International Creative Management, Inc., 40 West 57th Street, New York, NY 10019. Attn: Sarah Jane Leigh.

SPECIAL NOTE
Anyone receiving permission to produce APARTMENT 3A is required to give credit to the Author as sole and exclusive Author of the Play on the title page of all programs distributed in connection with performances of the Play and in all instances in which the title of the Play appears for purposes of advertising, publicizing or otherwise exploiting the Play and/or a production thereof. The name of the Author must appear on a separate line, in which no other name appears, immediately beneath the title and in size of type equal to 50% of the size of the largest, most prominent letter used for the title of the Play. No person, firm or entity may receive credit larger or more prominent than that accorded the Author. The following acknowledgment must appear on the title page in all programs distributed in connection with performances of the Play:

Originally produced by the Purple Rose Theatre Company (1996)
Jeff Daniels, Executive Director
Guy Sanville, Artistic Director
Alan Ribant, Managing Director

APARTMENT 3A premiered at the Purple Rose Theatre Company (Guy Sanville, Artistic Director; Jeff Daniels, Executive Director; Alan Ribant, Managing Director) in Chelsea, Michigan, on October 4, 1996. It was directed by Guy Sanville; the set design was by Dan Walker; the lighting design was by Dana White; the sound design was by R. Thomas Bray; the costume design was by Christina M. Foster; and the stage manager was Anthony Caselli. The cast was as follows:

ANNIE .... Suzi Regan
DAL .... Leo McNamara
DONALD .... Randall Godwin
ELLIOT .... Joseph Albright
TONY .... Anthony Caselli

CHARACTERS

ANNIE — thirties
DAL — fifties or sixties
DONALD — late thirties
ELLIOT — thirties
TONY — thirties or forties

PLACE

The place is in and around Annie's life in a city of some size
in the Midwest.

TIME

The time is now and then.

APARTMENT 3A

ACT ONE

As the house lights fade out, we hear a cellist playing a waltz of some kind. The lights fade up on an empty apartment in a Midwestern city. Night. Wood floor, one upstage window, one door and two mismatched chairs sit facing each other around a plain wooden table.

The cellist fades down but not out, now coming from somewhere distant, as if in an apartment above and over this one. A siren is heard passing below the window. Several beats of stillness as the cellist continues to play. Two voices are approaching.

DAL. You're one lucky lady, that's all I gotta say.

ANNIE. I'm glad I saw the sign.

DAL. Yeah, and now where are ya?

ANNIE. I'm sorry?

DAL. I says, and now where are ya?

ANNIE. I'm right here.

DAL. And where's all the people who ain't here? They're somewhere else, that's where. Lucky for you, unlucky for them. And if you decide to take this place, which if you're smart you will, pity me 'cause my phone is gonna ring off the hook from all of them wanting to know, what about 3A, what happened to 3A ...

ANNIE. It must be quite a place. *(The door opens and Annie enters, followed by Dal. Annie clutches a large shoulder bag.)*

DAL. Well, like anything, expect nothing and ye shall be rewarded. *(Annie surveys the apartment quickly before disappearing into the kitchen.)* Light and airy. Running water. Electrics. Bathroom. Kitchen. Walls are newly painted. If you don't — *(Annie returns, goes to look out the window.)* — like the color, we can negotiate, long as you're willing to do the work yourself.

ANNIE.   Not much of a view.

DAL.   Huh?

ANNIE.   I said, there's not much of a view.

DAL.   Well, it's night.

ANNIE.   I know that.

DAL.   You want a view, you're gonna have to wait 'til morning.

ANNIE.   It's just — no, I mean, I can see enough to know that it's kind of — I mean, it's fine, don't get me wrong. It's just that it looks like …

DAL.   A slum?

ANNIE.   In a word.

DAL.   Apparently, you have not heard the news. The state and the city are working together.

ANNIE.   Really.

DAL.   The governor. The mayor. Got together, talked it over. Decided to pour more money than you can shake a fist at into this city. And one of the places that's gonna see some of that jack is right outside that window.

ANNIE.   I thought the governor and the mayor weren't speaking.

DAL.   Oh, they're speakin'.

ANNIE.   No, I believe they're in the middle of a huge public feud. It's been on the front page of the paper for weeks now.

DAL.   That's all show. Anything that means anything never happens out where you can see it. It's always in a back room somewhere. Do yourself a big damn favor and take another look. What do ya see.

ANNIE.   I see a slum. At night.

DAL.   I'll tell ya what I see. I see the most beautiful public park in the history of this city. "A public park to be proud of," is how the governor will put it. The mayor will call it, "a place where people from all over the state will come to picnic."

ANNIE.   You're desperate to rent this place, aren't you?

DAL.   Not as desperate as you are.

ANNIE. You're right. I'll take it.

DAL. I'll need your first month's rent and one month's security.

ANNIE. I'll go to the bank first thing in the morning.

DAL. That's fine. When would you like to move in?

ANNIE. Tonight.

DAL. Tonight?

ANNIE. Is that a problem?

DAL. Not for me.

ANNIE. Good. *(Dal sets the keys down on the table.)*

DAL. If you want the cable hooked up, I'll send Betty up to the roof tomorrow to fiddle with the wires.

ANNIE. No, that's okay.

DAL. You don't want the cable?

ANNIE. No, I work for public television.

DAL. What's that?

ANNIE. Y'know, Channel 68?

DAL. Is it on the cable?

ANNIE. It's near the end of the, y'know. Near the end. 65, 66, 67 …

DAL. 68.

ANNIE. That's us.

DAL. Can't say that I've seen it. Course, me and Betty stick pretty much to the Disney Channel. The rest of it's just shit. *(Mimes flicking a remote.)* Shit. Shit. Shit. Shit. Disney. Pardon my French.

ANNIE. Well, if Disney ever lets you down, give us a try. *(Dal picks up a small paint brush, looks at it.)*

DAL. You have any problems with anything, call my wife.

ANNIE. I will.

DAL. In the morning. By the afternoon, she's, y'know … *(Dal mimes drinking.)*

ANNIE. Got it.

DAL. I'll leave you to yourself. It's the best apartment in the building. Treat it nice.

ANNIE. I will. Good night.

DAL. G'night now. *(Annie shuts the door. After several beats of silence, she turns and slides down to the floor and cries. A sharp knock is heard.)*

ANNIE. Jesus!

DONALD. *(O.S.)* No, it's Donald. Donald Peterson? I live in 3B across the hall? I just wanted to pop over, say hello, introduce myself. I know it's late, I'm sorry, I don't mean to bother you. Is now a bad time?

ANNIE. Yes, it is.

DONALD. *(O.S.)* Sometimes moving into a new place can be very isolating. Just wanted to throw out the welcome mat.

ANNIE. Please come back tomorrow.

DONALD. *(O.S.)* What was that? I'm sorry?

ANNIE. Please come back tomorrow.

DONALD. *(O.S.)* Tomorrow?

ANNIE. Yes.

DONALD. *(O.S.)* What time?

ANNIE. What?

DONALD. *(O.S.)* What time tomorrow would you like me to come back?

ANNIE. Nine.

DONALD. *(O.S.)* In the morning?

ANNIE. Yes.

DONALD. *(O.S.)* How about nine-thirty? I have to be someplace at nine. I'm not sure I can make it.

ANNIE. Nine-thirty then.

DONALD. *(O.S.)* Perfect. I'll see you then.

ANNIE. See you then.

DONALD. *(O.S.)* Oh, did Dal offer to have Betty hook up your cable?

ANNIE. Yes, he did.

DONALD. *(O.S.)* Make sure you get her in the morning. By afternoon, she's —

ANNIE. I know. He told me. Thank you. Good night.

DONALD. *(O.S.)* Good night. *(Annie gets up, crosses D. to the dresser with her purse. Just as she is about to reach the dresser, the door swings open. Donald stands there, thirties, slender, not unattractive. He wears a beautifully tailored suit.)* Oops. I'm sorry. Your door was unlocked. You really shouldn't do that. It's not that great a neighborhood.

ANNIE. What are you doing?

8

DONALD. I'm leaving. I just heard Dal's voice, figured he was showing the apartment. I couldn't help myself. I love this apartment. Don't you just love it?

ANNIE. Look, it was nice meeting you. *(Donald goes to the D. "window.")*

DONALD. Oh, would you look at that! Y'know, someday that's going to be a park. Apparently, the governor and the mayor are going to have a picnic.

ANNIE. So I've heard.

DONALD. No, this is definitely the penthouse. If you don't think so, come on over and see where I'm at.

ANNIE. Yeah, well, maybe another time.

DONALD. You're going to love this building. Moved here three years ago. Was it three years? Three years ago. My wife's job changed. No. Sorry. She "relocated." God, she'd kill me if she heard me say that. She's a securities broker. "Makes her living trading other people's insecurities," as she says. She's funny. You'd like her. Right now she's in Rome. Not living, just on business. She loves it there. She says it's like heaven on earth.

ANNIE. Really.

DONALD. Oh, yes. We started out in the States. First there was Boston. Then Los Angeles. Then came Washington. The capitol, not the state. *(Donald makes his way to the table, fingering one of the chairs.)*

ANNIE. Right.

DONALD. Then Tokyo. Followed by six months in Frankfurt. She hated Frankfurt. Have you ever been to Frankfurt?

ANNIE. No.

DONALD. If you ever go, stay away from the sausages, they're hallucinogenic. Right now, she's in Rome.

ANNIE. You told me.

DONALD. Oh. Sorry. I'm bothering you. I don't mean to. I'll leave you alone. It was nice meeting you, 3A.

ANNIE. It was nice meeting you, 3B.

DONALD. It's the best apartment in the building. Treat it nice. *(Donald goes out the door, Elliot enters, looking over papers. Neither notices the other. An office.)*

9

ELLIOT. Opening remarks via Larry. Looks like the standard plea for help. He stops just short of begging. You want me to go through it, take out the drama? … Annie?

ANNIE. What?

ELLIOT. *(Papers.)* Larry?

ANNIE. Just leave it.

ELLIOT. Why don't I just leave it. *(Elliot tosses the papers on the table. During the following, Annie begins changing. Hanging up her coat, getting another, pulling her hair back.)* There's a nasty rumor going around about you. Is it true?

ANNIE. Word travels fast.

ELLIOT. I'm sorry.

ANNIE. But not surprised.

ELLIOT. The only thing I'm surprised about is that you hung on for as long as you did.

ANNIE. You never liked him, did you?

ELLIOT. Who?

ANNIE. Richard.

ELLIOT. Oh, Richard. Right. I never could remember his name.

ANNIE. Thank you.

ELLIOT. If there's anything I can do.

ANNIE. Well, for starters, you can tell me why I keep falling in love with men who treat me like shit.

ELLIOT. I don't think that's necessarily your fault.

ANNIE. Why do we do this to ourselves, Elliot?

ELLIOT. Why do you date men who treat you like shit or why do we work for public broadcasting?

ANNIE. Yes.

ELLIOT. Well, seeing how I forgot to bring my ten-foot pole, we work at Channel 68 because it's important. Because whether people know it or not, their lives would be less without us and are more because of us. Because of what we do —

ANNIE. Blah, blah.

ELLIOT. — their quality of life is enriched, enhanced and expanded —

ANNIE. Blah, blah —

ELLIOT. — and, in the end, saved from falling into the black hole of banality that threatens what is left of cultural society.

ANNIE. — blah, blah, blah, blah, blah. You just toe that company line, don't you?

ELLIOT. Yes, I do. But I also believe every word of it. And so do you.

ANNIE. Do you watch public television?

ELLIOT. What?

ANNIE. Do you?

ELLIOT. You mean ... actually watch it?

ANNIE. Do you turn on your television set with the express purpose of watching a selected program on Channel 68? Yes or no.

ELLIOT. If you're asking if I watched that documentary on the mating habits of the Siberian Polar Bear, the answer is yes, as a matter of fact, I did. Why, didn't you?

ANNIE. No, I'm afraid I missed that one. *(Annie sits, taking a tube of lipstick out of her purse.)*

ELLIOT. Too bad. I found it very educational.

ANNIE. Why does that scare me?

ELLIOT. They had such grace and beauty. And commitment. And passion for each other. I mean, at times I forgot they were ... well, bears. In fact ... never mind.

ANNIE. What?

ELLIOT. As strange as this may sound, they also had surprisingly good technique. *(Off Annie's look.)* Swear to God! They were making moves on each other.

ANNIE. And you were what, taking notes?

ELLIOT. No, of course not. But I couldn't help but be, y'know ...

ANNIE. Enriched, enhanced and expanded?

ELLIOT. In a very pure, primal, non-bestiality kind of way, yes. I felt like a voyeur. I mean, to be able to sit there in the comfort of my own living room and watch two extremely large mammals boink each other's brains out on the frozen tundra ... I'm sorry, but you just don't get quality television like that anymore.

ANNIE. And I wonder why we have to have pledge drives.

ELLIOT. Oh, here we go.

ANNIE. What?

ELLIOT. You're doing it again.

ANNIE. No, I'm not.

ELLIOT. Yes, you are. You do it every time.

ANNIE.   This is different!

ELLIOT.   Every year, it's "nobody cares, nobody gives a shit —

ANNIE.   They don't care, Elliot! And they —

ELLIOT.   — anymore, nothing matters."

ANNIE.   — don't give a shit! We're non-essential! We're like asparagus. We're good for you, but who in their right mind wants to eat us?

ELLIOT.   People believe in what we do, Annie. They just need to be reminded.

ANNIE.   Well then, you tell me how I'm supposed to get the five-year olds who watch *Sesame Street* to pick up their phones and pledge to Channel 68 because those are the people I'm going to be talking to here in less than — *(Checks watch.)* — shit! I gotta go! Where's Larry's copy? Oh God —

ELLIOT.   Right here.

ANNIE.   — oh God, oh God, oh God!

ELLIOT.   You'll do fine.

ANNIE.   Quick! Tell me something wonderful about myself! *(Elliot thinks.)* C'mon!

ELLIOT.   Okay, okay. Remember when you first came to work here? You hadn't even been here a week, you were here a week, and you were standing on top of my desk, screaming at the top of your lungs about how we were going to "change the face of public broadcasting locally, nationally and —

ANNIE.   *(With Elliot.)* Nationally and across the world!

ELLIOT.   — across the world!" That's right.

ANNIE.   Kenneth Branagh in *Henry V!* I thought if he could do it, so could I!

ELLIOT.   Well, it worked. We'd have followed you anywhere. Some of us still will.

ANNIE.   Thank you!

ELLIOT.   You're welcome. *(Annie marches past Elliot who hands her the papers. Annie looks them over quickly as the lights change. A "WPBK Channel 68" logo appears. A TV studio.)* Listen, I was thinking. Now that things, y'know, now that your situation has changed, I was wondering if maybe we could —

ANNIE.   *(Papers)* This is shit.

VOICE/TONY.   *(Offstage, intercom.)* Ten seconds to air.

ANNIE. Did Larry write this? This is terrible. I can't say this. *(Elliot attaches a microphone to Annie's lapel.)*
ELLIOT. Wing it, Kenneth.
VOICE/TONY. *(O.S.)* Five, four, three, two — have a good one! *(Elliot moves into the shadows behind Annie, his back to the audience, as if talking with those working the phone bank. Annie turns to an imaginary camera, instantly calm.)*
ANNIE. *(To unseen camera.)* Welcome. Welcome and hello. My name is Annie Wilson and I'm WPBK's Director of Fundraising here at Channel 68. Before we go back to Big Bird and all of his wonderful friends on *Sesame Street*, we're going to take a short little break for just a couple minutes, because we have to do something that's very, very important. How many Big Bird fans do we have out there? Let me see you raise your hands? Oh, my! So many of you! That's great. Y'know, Big Bird and his friends like you just as much as you like them and I know all of my friends behind me love Big Bird and all of his friends, too. Don't you? *(Annie turns to Elliot, who gives a quick thumbs up.)* Yes, indeed. But unfortunately, bringing *Sesame Street* into your home costs money. And that's why we're here. Channel 68 needs your help. If there are any of you parents out there who are watching *Sesame Street* along with your children, you may have noticed there are no commercials on public broadcasting. Instead of selling advertising spots that would break up our programming, we rely on the help of you, our viewers, big and small. That's why these wonderful people are behind me poised over their telephones. They are waiting for you to pick up your phone and make a donation that will make sure Big Bird and all his friends on *Sesame Street* can keep coming into your home every morning. Because if they couldn't … if they couldn't that would be … that would be bad. B-A-D, bad, boys and girls. Because … okay. All right. Here it is. You know what's going to happen if no one calls? Do you have any idea what will happen if those phones don't ring? There will be no more *Sesame Street*. And no more *Sesame Street* means no Big Bird. No Bert and Ernie. No Oscar. No Cookie Monster. No Mr. Snuffleupagus. All of your friends on *Sesame Street* will be gone. That's what will happen, boys and girls, if those phones don't ring. Because without Channel 68, Big Bird and all of his friends will be dead. And …

you know what dead is, don't you, boys and girls? Dead is gone. Dead is — *(Phones start ringing.)* — goodbye. Dead is someplace you don't want to go. Someplace you don't want to be. Something you wouldn't wish on anyone. Except for certain right-wing extremists on Capitol Hill who think public television isn't worthy of federal funding and military bands are. *(The sound of many phones ringing.)* Are those phones I hear ringing? Why, I think they are. But wait, I think I still see a few of you boys and girls just sitting there. Don't be shy. Just walk over, pick up your phone and call us at 1-800-555-WPBK. And if you're too young to dial the number yourself, don't cry. Just go get one of your parents and tell them, "Please, Mommy and Daddy. Help save Big Bird. Call Channel 68 and make a pledge. Before it's too late." *(Annie holds a smile.)*

VOICE/TONY. *(O.S.)* And we're clear.

ELLIOT. Holy shit.

VOICE/TONY. *(O.S.)* Big Bird will be dead?

ELLIOT. Annie?

ANNIE. Yes?

ELLIOT. What was that?

ANNIE. That was me. Raising money. That's my job, remember?

VOICE/TONY. *(O.S.)* Big Bird will be dead?

ELLIOT. Did you clear it with Larry?

ANNIE. No, I did not clear it with Larry. I don't have to clear things with Larry.

ELLIOT. But don't you think in this case —

ANNIE. I had an idea and I ran with it, Elliot. It's what I do.

VOICE/TONY. *(O.S.)* Big Bird will be dead? *(Still heard over the intercom, Tony can now be seen standing up in the booth, screaming at Annie from behind the glass.)*

ANNIE. Yes, Tony! Big Bird will be dead and so will we! That's the point!

TONY. *(Booth.)* You can't kill Big Bird!

ANNIE. I'm not killing, who said anything about killing Big Bird?

TONY. *(Booth, to someone unseen.)* Did we just violate —

ANNIE. Look, can't you hear the phones? Can you —

TONY. *(Booth.)* — an FCC regulation? Somebody find out if we just violated an FCC regulation! Annie, you want to —

ANNIE. — hear phones ringing, Tony? I hear phones ringing!

TONY. *(Booth.)* — tell me what the hell you think you're doing?

ANNIE. I'm trying to save the station! What the hell —

TONY. *(Booth.)* By what, scaring the shit out of innocent children?

ANNIE. — do you think, what are you talking about? What are you talking about, there is no such thing as an innocent child anymore! I can't —

TONY. *(Booth, to someone unseen.)* Get my wife on the phone! Find out —

ANNIE. — scare them. They know more about —

TONY. *(Booth.)* — if my kids are okay. I don't believe this.

ANNIE. — what's going on in the world than half the fucking adults in this country! You don't think they don't know Big Bird is going to die? They know he's going to die, they just don't know — *(Annie disappears inside the booth. Annie and Tony can be seen arguing through the glass. Elliot sits against the table, smiling.)*

TONY. *(Booth.)* Big Bird is not going to die, what are you — what the hell do you think you're doing? Get out of here! You can't be in here! This is the booth! This is my booth! Don't come into my booth and scream at me! Don't come into my booth and —

ANNIE. *(Booth.)* — of what? Maybe AIDS? Maybe he'll die of AIDS? Or leukemia? Or how about cancer? Or something even more random like getting gunned down by a gang or being the victim of a drive-by shooting or a drug deal gone bad! A car jacking, sodomy, rape, a plane crash, a drunk driver — *(Tony backs Annie out of the booth. Elliot goes to Annie and begins to pull her back down.)* — welfare reform, malnutrition or maybe his Daddy molested him! His Mommy molested him! His Mommy and Daddy both molested him!

TONY. — scream at me! Yeah, right, that's great! That's just great! Y'know, you've gone too far, you know that? This time you've gone too far! I'm not backing you up this time! You're on your own, Annie! You want to go down, go down by yourself! Jesus! Where's — *(Tony goes back into the booth. Booth.)* — Larry! Get me Larry! *(To Annie.)* Yeah, you're right! You're always right!

(To someone unseen.) Try his car! Goddammit, I hope he wasn't watching *Sesame Street* this morning! *(Tony slams the door. Lights change. Annie's office.)*

ANNIE.   Don't say it.

ELLIOT.   I wasn't going to say anything.

ANNIE.   You don't have to. I already know.

ELLIOT.   You took a chance. Nothing wrong with that.

ANNIE.   I care too much.

ELLIOT.   Yeah well, somebody has to.

ANNIE.   Well, I wish it were somebody other than me. Do yourself a favor, Elliot. When the shit hits the fan, duck.

ELLIOT.   Well, that's going to be kind of tough. *(Off Annie's look.)* I made reservations at Piccolo's for lunch. Three and a half stars, table for two right in the corner. Just what the doctor ordered.

ANNIE.   I am the last person you want to have lunch with.

ELLIOT.   That's not true. I've wanted to have lunch with you ever since the day you stood on my desk.

ANNIE.   Elliot.

ELLIOT.   It's just a lunch, Annie.

ANNIE.   No, it's not. It's more than that.

ELLIOT.   Yeah, I guess it is.

ANNIE.   I'm sorry. I'm just not ready for lunch right now.

ELLIOT.   Of course, you aren't. It's nine-thirty in the morning. I was thinking more like noon.

ANNIE.   No.

ELLIOT.   Or one, two —

ANNIE.   Elliot.

ELLIOT.   — three, four, we're into dinner now, five, six —

ANNIE.   That's not what I meant.

ELLIOT.   I know that's not what you meant. I'm just standing here trying to get out of this with at least some sort of dignity.

ANNIE.   I'm sorry.

ELLIOT.   I understand. Really.

ANNIE.   Maybe another time.

ELLIOT.   Another time. I got some stuff I gotta do, so I'm just gonna …

ANNIE.   Right.

ELLIOT. You okay?

ANNIE. I'm fine. *(Elliot starts to leave.)*

ELLIOT. Oh. Just so you know? I thought what you did out there was one of the bravest things I've ever seen in the history of this station. *(As Elliot goes out the door, Dal enters. Neither notices the other. Donald, carrying a bag of groceries, wanders in behind Dal.)*

DAL. You left your door open again.

ANNIE. What?

DAL. Your door.

ANNIE. Right. Sorry.

DAL. If this were a barn, you'd be outta horses. Here. *(Dal hands Annie a key.)* Just had Betty put a new lock on the front door. Somebody broke in last night.

ANNIE. What?

DAL. Spray-painted profanity up and down the fifth floor stairwell.

ANNIE. Someone broke into the building?

DAL. Goddamn, shitfaced, asshole crackheads is my guess. Pardon my French.

ANNIE. How? I mean, how'd they get in?

DAL. They broke in.

ANNIE. I know that, but how? I mean, when? When did this happen?

DAL. Last night, this morning, hard to say. Ain't no keepin' 'em out. They wanna get in, they're gonna get in, new lock or no new lock. But leavin' your door open is like puttin' out a big, fat welcome mat for trouble.

ANNIE. Don't worry. I'll keep it shut.

DAL. And locked.

ANNIE. And locked.

DAL. Not that it'll do any good. You changed your mind about the cable yet?

ANNIE. No, I haven't. Did you call the police?

DAL. The police won't do nothin' 'cept tell ya to keep your door locked.

ANNIE. Well, we should still call them, don't you think? *(Dal goes off.)*

17

DAL.   Lemme know when you want the cable.

ANNIE.   Dal? Shouldn't we at least report it to the police?

DONALD.   Nobody broke in.

ANNIE.   What?

DONALD.   Nobody broke in.

ANNIE.   But he just said ...

DONALD.   It was an inside job.

ANNIE.   You mean somebody in the building?

DONALD.   Betty.

ANNIE.   Betty?

DONALD.   Yesterday. I saw her walking up the stairs. Can of spray paint in each hand, mumbling various obscenities.

ANNIE.   Why would she do that?

DONALD.   Are you kidding? She probably doesn't even remember it.

ANNIE.   Oh God, that's so sad. Is she really that bad?

DONALD.   Only in the afternoons.

ANNIE.   Well, if I see her coming towards me with a can of spray paint and it's afternoon, I'll lock my door.

DONALD.   *(With Annie.)* Lock your door, that's probably a good idea. *(Pause.)*

ANNIE.   Well, it was good to see you again.

DONALD.   You, too. Oh, do you mind if I ask you something?

ANNIE.   Sure.

DONALD.   Is Big Bird really going to die?

ANNIE.   Yes, I'm afraid so.

DONALD.   How sad.

ANNIE.   Yes. Yes, it is.

DONALD.   Maybe it's his time to go.

ANNIE.   Or hers.

DONALD.   Or hers, right.

ANNIE.   We're not sure which ...

DONALD.   Well, regardless, I'll have to send in a contribution. I just hope it's not too late.

ANNIE.   On behalf of everyone at *Sesame Street*, I thank you.

DONALD.   On behalf of those who are too traumatized for words mainly because they're less than five years old and can't speak in complete sentences yet, you're welcome.

ANNIE.   If it means our station will live to see another year, it's worth rockin' their little world.

DONALD.   That kind of belief in something is admirable.

ANNIE.   Right. Well. *(Annie at the door.)* I'm going to lock my door now.

DONALD.   Do you like eggs?

ANNIE.   I'm sorry?

DONALD.   They say the world is divided into two kinds of people. Those who like eggs and those who don't. Me? I happen to love them.

ANNIE.   That's nice.

DONALD.   What about you?

ANNIE.   What about me what?

DONALD.   Which side do you come down on?

ANNIE.   I don't know.

DONALD.   You have to know. You're either one or the other.

ANNIE.   I don't know what I am.

DONALD.   Are you for or against?

ANNIE.   I like eggs.

DONALD.   Whew, that's a relief. Because I was just at the market and I happened to pick up two dozen Grade A Large in the hopes that you didn't have any plans for dinner.

ANNIE.   Dinner?

DONALD.   If you're worried about my cooking ability, don't. I've been told by people who've eaten in restaurants, I'm not bad.

ANNIE.   Wait a minute.

DONALD.   In fact, I'll make you something I guarantee you're going to love. It's nothing short of a miracle. I call it, "Scrambled Eggs à la Donald." It's a French dish.

ANNIE.   I'm sure it's delicious. But I can't tonight, I'm sorry. I have to work.

DONALD.   Liar.

ANNIE.   I beg your pardon?

DONALD.   I said, you're lying. It's okay. I'd rather catch you at it now and tell you to your face then to go on knowing it happened but neither one of us was willing to deal with it.

ANNIE.   I have work to do tonight.

19

DONALD.   Tell you what. Why don't I make enough for both of us and when it's ready I'll come over, knock twice and leave it outside your door.

ANNIE.   Excuse me. Just a second. Let me make this as clear as possible. Okay?

DONALD.   I'm a big fan of clarity.

ANNIE.   Good. There is nothing that's going to happen between us.

DONALD.   What do you mean?

ANNIE.   I mean, we happen to be neighbors. And that's it. That's all we're going to be. Get it?

DONALD.   Oh.

ANNIE.   Do we understand each other?

DONALD.   Absolutely.

ANNIE.   Good.

DONALD.   We're not going to have sex.

ANNIE.   No. We're not.

DONALD.   Good. Because that will be a big relief to my wife. You know I'm married, don't you?

ANNIE.   You told me.

DONALD.   Happily.

ANNIE.   Yeah, right. Whatever.

DONALD.   No, I really am. I have a picture of her. You want to see it? She's beautiful. Here. Hold this. (Donald shoves the groceries into Annie's arms.)

ANNIE.   No, I don't want —

DONALD.   You can see for yourself just how beautiful she is.

ANNIE.   — to see, Jesus.

DONALD.   I took it a few years ago, but she hasn't aged a day. Here it is. I got it right here. (Displays picture.) See?

ANNIE.   She's beautiful.

DONALD.   Told you.

ANNIE.   No, she is. She's stunning.

DONALD.   I know what you're thinking.

ANNIE.   I'm not thinking anything.

DONALD.   Yes, you are. What is someone like her doing with somebody like me?

ANNIE.   That wasn't either what I was thinking.

DONALD.   Liar.

ANNIE.   Would you not do that, please?

DONALD.   Then tell the truth.

ANNIE.   Look. Donald. You have a beautiful wife. I'm happy for you. But I still don't want to have dinner with you. What I want is to be left alone.

DONALD.   Why would you possibly want to be alone?

ANNIE.   All right, that's it. I'm getting Dal. *(Donald stops Annie with a simple gesture.)*

DONALD.   For your information, aside from me and Dal and Betty, the only people in this building are seven very depressed retirees, a couple of first-year residents from the hospital who are never here, a sex pad down on two which gets used every month and a half by some insurance adjuster from Illinois and a cellist up on five whom I love to listen to but have yet to meet. You're the first person I've seen come through here in a long time who resembles someone I might be the least bit interested in getting to know. And when I say getting to know, I don't mean scrambled eggs today, taking showers together tomorrow. Though I'd be an idiot if I didn't say that yes, I do find you attractive but no, I am not going to leave my stunningly beautiful wife for you no matter how many tricks you might be able to do with a bar of soap. And there's no use in trying to talk me out of it. I am hopelessly in love with the woman in my wallet and there's nothing you can say or do to change that. Which is why, when I saw your door open I wanted to do two things and two things only. I wanted to see if you would be interested in sampling the best scrambled eggs you'll ever eat and in getting my own personal update on Big Bird's condition. You'll notice that nowhere in there did anyone mention anything about ruining your life. Which, from the looks of it, could use some eggs.

ANNIE.   I'm sorry.

DONALD.   No, you're not. You're just scared of something I promise you has nothing to do with me. Maybe another time. *(Donald picks up the bag of groceries and starts out.)*

ANNIE.   Yes. *(Donald stops at the door.)* Yes, I'm one of those people who like eggs. And yes, I would love it if you would stay and make me your Scrambled Eggs à la Donald.

DONALD.   Under one condition.

ANNIE.   I know. If I hate them, I have to be honest.

DONALD.   No, if you hate them, for God's sake, lie to my face, please, it's my best dish. No, you have to promise in order for this platonic, howdy neighbor, can-I-borrow-a-cup-of-sugar thing to have any chance of lasting at all that, no matter what, you cannot under any circumstances, fall in love with me. *(Annie tries to hold back a laugh.)* I couldn't be more serious. *(Annie laughs. Donald begins to unpack a bottle of wine and two glasses.)* Fortunately, my high self-esteem saves me from being forever scarred by your callous disregard for my feelings.

ANNIE.   *(Laughing.)* I'm sorry!

DONALD.   Liar.

ANNIE.   You're right! *(Donald disappears into the kitchen.)*

DONALD.   *(O.S.)* You think I'm kidding but trust me, I've seen it happen. There was this woman who used to live in the building. Swedish girl by the name of Inga.

ANNIE.   Inga?

DONALD.   *(O.S.)* Every time I went down to check my mail, Inga was there waiting at the mailbox. And then, one day, for no apparent reason whatever, she mounted me.

ANNIE.   Mounted you?

DONALD.   *(O.S.)* As if she were getting on a horse. It's true. I almost whinnied. Or nayed, I'm not sure what. It didn't matter because before I knew it — *(Donald enters with a wine opener.)* — Inga was feeling up every part of my body.

ANNIE.   Really.

DONALD.   Oh, yes. She had her hands in places I'd never touched. She was insatiable. Voracious. Couldn't be stopped. Six weeks later, I said, "I've had just about enough of this."

ANNIE.   What about your wife?

DONALD.   She was in Frankfurt at the time, thank God.

ANNIE.   Lucky for you. *(Donald pours the wine and hands Annie a glass.*

DONALD.   Very lucky for me. She hated Frankfurt. If you ever go, stay away from the sausages, they're hallucinogenic.

ANNIE.   You told me.

DONALD.   Did I? I'm sorry.

ANNIE. It's all right.

DONALD. You'll have to forgive me. When it comes to my wife, I'm afraid I forget myself. "My wife's a securities broker for Merrill Lynch, everybody gather round!" She's over in Rome right now.

ANNIE. Right.

DONALD. I told you that.

ANNIE. Yes.

DONALD. Hmm. I'm going to visit her soon. Have I mentioned that yet?

ANNIE. No, you haven't. *(Donald sits with his glass of wine.)*

DONALD. Whew. Usually, I don't go. Usually, I stay home. I have my own projects. Things I'm doing.

ANNIE. Like what?

DONALD. I paint. Watercolors.

ANNIE. Really.

DONALD. Hm-hmm.

ANNIE. I tried that once. Didn't have the patience. Though I must say, I did enjoy painting all those naked college boys. *(Donald refills her glass.)*

DONALD. I'm into landscapes, mostly. I went through a sort of pseudo-impressionist period where I thought I was Cezanne until I realized there's only one of him every hundred years. So I went back to my barns and sunsets and bouquets of flowers. Y'know, nothing to threaten the art world as we know it.

ANNIE. Have you been shown anywhere?

DONALD. Yes, my work in on permanent display in my apartment.

ANNIE. I see.

DONALD. Tickets are very inexpensive. Free, actually. And yet still, no one seems to come. Odd.

ANNIE. Except for your wife.

DONALD. Well, besides her, of course. But then, she's nothing if not supportive. Especially, after I painted her. She was sitting in the window of this little cottage we had a few summers ago. And she turned away from the window and was looking right at me. The sun was just pouring in, drenching her in this waterfall of light, dark browns and deep reds bouncing right off her hair onto my canvas. I swear it painted itself. What makes it so wonderful, so forever … well, it's my best work.

ANNIE.   I'd like to see it.

DONALD.   What about you? Tell me something about you.

ANNIE.   There's nothing to tell.

DONALD.   Tell me why you were crying the other night.

ANNIE.   I wasn't crying.

DONALD.   Liar.

ANNIE.   Don't do that.

DONALD.   Then tell the truth.

ANNIE.   I don't know you well enough.

DONALD.   You don't know me at all. But that's probably a good thing because it'll make it easier. I won't be judging you or telling you why you're wrong or what you should have done or could've done or what I would've done. I'll just listen. Like a good neighbor should.

ANNIE.   I came home. I was early. And there he was. Or there should I say was his bare ass because that's all I could see. That and her legs wrapped around his back. Actually, they were way up around his neck. And I remember thinking, what's Richard doing fucking a gymnast on top of my grandmother's dining room table. I actually stood there, marveling at their flexibility. Mary Lou saw me first. Oh, my God. Richard. Richard. He turns. He sees. Lots of silence. Lots of fumbling for clothing no one can find. He tries to apologize. He tries to make it my fault. He tries to get me to slap him. Hit him. Hate him. All I want to do is to check the condition of my grandmother's table. She leaves. I go into the kitchen. I come back out with some furniture polish and I make what I thought was the love of my fucking life polish that table until it shines. The next morning, I put it out on the street and it's gone in thirty minutes. As is he. Cross fade. Two weeks later. I'm in the corner market. Richard walks in. With her. I say, Richard. He says, Annie. I say, what are you doing here. He says, picking up a few things. I can't resist. "You mean, besides her?" She calls me a bitch. Heads turn. The kid behind the counter looks up. I turn to Richard and say, why. All I want is a reason why. And he looks at me and he says … he says, because you care too much in a world that doesn't give a shit anymore … and I stand there, in

24

the middle of that market and for the first time in my life, I can't think of a thing to say. So I run. Out of my market. Out of my neighborhood. Out of my life as I know it. I end up at my local U-Haul outlet where I rent a truck for the first time in my life, pack up everything I own and start driving around the city in circles until I come upon this sign. Apartment For Rent. Which I do. After being told how lucky I am. *(Annie sips her wine.)*

DONALD. For what it's worth, I think you're one of the luckiest people I've ever met.

ANNIE. Liar.

DONALD. It's the truth. Y'know, they say there are only two kinds of people in this world.

ANNIE. You told me. Those who like eggs and those who don't.

DONALD. No, I just told you that so you'd have dinner with me. Two kinds of people. Those who know how to waltz and those who don't. Which are you?

ANNIE. I don't have a clue how to waltz.

DONALD. Well, that's good. Neither do I. *(Donald gets up.)* C'mon. On your feet.

ANNIE. What? *(Donald holds out his hand.)*

DONALD. Waltz with me.

ANNIE. Uh, no. I don't think so.

DONALD. C'mon. You need to have some fun.

ANNIE. I'm not going to waltz with you, Donald.

DONALD. Okay. I was hoping it wouldn't come to this. *(Donald begins waltzing around the room.)* One, two, three. One, two, three. One …

ANNIE. Excuse me. Excuse me.

DONALD. … two, three. One, two, three. One, two …

ANNIE. What are you doing?

DONALD. Waltzing. Alone.

ANNIE. Could you not do that, please?

DONALD. Sorry. I'm one of those people who once I start something, I can't stop.

ANNIE. Donald, please.

DONALD. One, two, three. One, two —

ANNIE. Donald. Donald!

DONALD. — three. One, two, three. One, two —

25

ANNIE. All right, all right! I'll waltz with you! *(Donald stops.)* I don't believe this. *(Slightly drunk, Annie gets up and goes to Donald. Donald places her hands in the proper position, gently kicking her feet wider apart.)* I can't dance without music.

DONALD. Do you have any waltzing CDs?

ANNIE. No.

DONALD. Wish us luck! And … one, two, three. One, two, three … *(Donald takes a big step as does Annie. Towards each other. They bump hard.)* Why don't I lead? And … one, two, three. One, two, three … *(Donald and Annie waltz around the apartment. Annie dances terribly. Donald isn't much better. Annie is hunched over, taking two steps to every one of Donald's. Their dancing is a disaster.)* … one, two, three. Big finish!, One, two, three … *(Donald spins Annie, who reels out of control. Donald holds her hand to keep her from falling into a heap.)* Sorry about that.

ANNIE. You okay?

DONALD. Fine. You?

ANNIE. Yeah. *(Annie pulls Donald into her. Hard. Back in position, ready for more.)*

DONALD. One, two, three … *(Donald and Annie continue during the following.)* … one, two, three. One, two, three. When my wife and I dance … she loves to waltz. And she's brilliant at it. Unfortunately, she married me. They tried to teach me, but it was hopeless. She enrolled us in one of those adult dance classes, where one night a week you meet in a room with a bunch of other dysfunctional steppers. Thanks to me, we were by far the worst of the worst. *(Donald clumsily spins Annie out of their embrace. Annie half crawls to her seat, holding her ankle.)* Oops.

ANNIE. I think I'll sit this one out.

DONALD. Anyway, when it — *(Donald brings Annie her wine glass.)* — came time for our final exam, right as we were about ready to go, she whispered into my ear. And the music started. "Can you hear the music?" And I said, yes. And then she started counting. "One, two, three. One, two, three. One, two, three." And off we went — *(Donald spins around the room by himself, dancing somewhat elegantly.)* — and it was like we were floating on air! We were Fred and Ginger! Spinning around and around the room! And that's when I knew — *(Donald collapses into a chair.*) — you truly haven't lived until you've waltzed with the one you love. *(Half exhausted, Donald picks up his wine glass.)* Sappy, huh?

ANNIE.   It's a lovely story. Excuse me, I have to get some ice for my ankle. *(Donald is up in an instant.)*

DONALD.   Oh, I'll get it.

ANNIE.   No, that's all right.

DONALD.   Don't be ridiculous. I injured you. Stay right there. It's the least I can do. *(Donald goes off with both glasses and the wine bottle.)*

ANNIE.   There's a blue ice bag under the sink!

DONALD.   *(O.S.)* Tell me about Elliot.

ANNIE.   Elliot?

DONALD.   *(O.S.)* That guy you kept looking back at during your little Big Bird address. *(Elliot enters through the door.)*

ELLIOT.   Larry's here and he's pissed.

ANNIE.   He's just this guy at work. Why?

DONALD.   *(O.S.)* Does he know how to waltz?

ANNIE.   What are you getting at?

ELLIOT.   We should get in there.

DONALD.   *(O.S.)* He looks like he'd be a good waltzer.

ANNIE.   *(To Donald.)* You're kidding. *(To Elliot.)* What's his mood?

ELLIOT.   Dark.

ANNIE.   How dark?

ELLIOT.   Dark dark.

ANNIE.   Larry, you wanted to see me? *(Lights change. Larry's office.)* Yes, I understand that, but I thought … I know but I thought the idea was to shake things … No, no one said, let's kill Big Bird. I understand that, but I thought by dealing with something kids could relate … it was just an idea, Larry. I ran with it. What do you want me to say? … Well, shit! We're all —

ELLIOT.   Annie.

ANNIE.   — walking around like we're gonna get pink slipped! This is exactly the time —

ELLIOT.   Annie, that's enough.

ANNIE.   — when we should be taking chances like — well then, fine! Fine! If that's what you think, then you've got your head up your ass further than I thought! *(Elliot steps in front of Annie.)*

27

ELLIOT. All right, that's it! Settle down, the both of you! Larry, I know you're concerned about what happened. Annie is obviously very passionate about this station, as am I. But I think it's important at a time like this, to find out the truth.

ANNIE. What are you talking about?

ELLIOT. Please. Larry? It was my idea. I told her to do it.

ANNIE. Elliot!

ELLIOT. I was the one who said, let's kill the bird.

ANNIE. That is not how it happened at all. I'm —

ELLIOT. Don't listen to her. You want to fire —

ANNIE. — sorry, that's not, what are you doing? What are —

ELLIOT. — somebody, Larry, fire me. But whatever you do, let Annie go free.

ANNIE. — you doing, Elliot? *(Lights change. Donald walks on with an ice bag. Elliot half freezes in place, still facing Larry.)*

DONALD. It's very Romeo and Juliet.

ANNIE. Well, that's Elliot. It doesn't matter. Once Larry saw the numbers from the first hour, he went crazy. Decided it was a brilliant idea to kill the bird. Naturally, Elliot tried to put his own noble spin on it.

ELLIOT. Larry, I lied. It was her idea. I hate myself. I'll start packing up my office. *(Elliot goes out the door.)*

DONALD. He quit?

ANNIE. God, no. Larry loves Elliot. Said public television needs more people like him. Apparently, the more martyrs, the merrier.

DONALD. And why is he so willing to sacrifice himself on your behalf?

ANNIE. I think he's in love with me.

DONALD. You think he's in love with you?

ANNIE. Well, I mean, I know he is.

DONALD. How do you know?

ANNIE. He asked me to lunch. *(Annie goes out to the kitchen.)*

DONALD. He what?

ANNIE. *(O.S.)* Made reservations and everything.

DONALD. He asked you out to lunch?

ANNIE. *(O.S.)* Hm-hmm.

DONALD.   And that means he's in love with you? *(Annie comes out of the kitchen with placemats, napkins and a breadbasket.)*
ANNIE.   Oh yeah. But I can't.
DONALD.   You can't what? Have lunch or fall in love?
ANNIE.   Both. You see, Elliot is one of these guys whom you look at ... I mean, there he is. You see him, you talk to him, but somehow he doesn't exist.
DONALD.   He's nondescript.
ANNIE.   He's very nondescript. He's so nondescript he disappears right before your eyes.
DONALD.   I just want to get this ...
ANNIE.   Sure.
DONALD.   Even though he throws himself at the mercy of your boss and admits to doing something you both know he didn't do, he can't win so much as a simple lunch? *(Annie goes to the dresser, takes out a sketch pad and sets it aside. During the following, she gets out some assorted silverware and brings it to the table.)*
ANNIE.   I'm doing him a huge favor, believe me.
DONALD.   How's that?
ANNIE.   Look, men with me flame out. If you're a man and you decide to enter into a relationship with me, you're going to find yourself starring in your own personal version of Oedipus. Before you know it, it's all just so many bleeding eye sockets. *(Annie begins laying out the silverware and breadbasket. Donald picks up the sketch pad.)*
DONALD.   So you're protecting him.
ANNIE.   I'm protecting myself. I think I've earned the right.
DONALD.   It might be easier all the way around if Elliot were a complete jerk.
ANNIE.   Are you kidding? I'd be buying him lunch.
DONALD.   Or a liar. If he lied to you, I can see how you might —
ANNIE.   Elliot's nothing if not truthful. And noble. Don't forget noble.
DONALD.   Inconsiderate?
ANNIE.   Nope.
DONALD.   Selfish?
ANNIE.   Forget it.
DONALD.   Sexist? Insensitive? Overly macho?

ANNIE.   None of the above. *(Donald sits with the sketch pad.)*
DONALD.   Hmm. Then it must be the idea of having sex with him.
ANNIE.   You don't waste any time, do you?
DONALD.   If you'd rather not talk about it.
ANNIE.   I would rather not talk about it.
DONALD.   Fine.
ANNIE.   I could have sex with Elliot. I could. Under certain conditions. Y'know, if it presented itself at the right time. At the right moment. And if there were a three-quarter moon with Venus rising and I had enough Chablis in me and the world were finally, truly, an ideal one, sex is an option I could explore with Elliot. *(Donald is sketching.)*
DONALD.   Again, if you'd rather not —
ANNIE.   Most of my relationships start out in the dark with soft music and no clothes on. Richard was a perfect example. I mean, it was only in the cold light of dawn that we made the decision to ask each other what our favorite colors were. Which, for me, turned out to be a lovely shade of abyss, thank you very much. And I'm not going to do that to Elliot. I'm not. He deserves better. Besides, I know what he really wants. He wants this lunch to be the first step towards dinner, followed by more dinners until, inevitably, he arrives at his ultimate goal which is, y'know …
DONALD.   Breakfast in bed?
ANNIE.   A life together.
DONALD.   Isn't that putting a little too much pressure on the midday meal?
ANNIE.   I think of it as dining defensively. From now on, I only eat lunch with someone who has the potential to be my Mr. Right. And Elliot is not my Mr. Right. He's not even my Mr. Half Right. He's not even my Mr. Half Right in the Right Sort of Light Right.
DONALD.   And you're sure about this?
ANNIE.   Positive.
DONALD.   One hundred percent.
ANNIE.   Yes.
DONALD.   No hope whatsoever. *(Annie holds up her fingers an inch apart.)*
ANNIE.   This much.

DONALD. Oh, so there's a chance.

ANNIE. No.

DONALD. You just said —

ANNIE. Okay, but that's like nothing.

DONALD. But it's still something.

ANNIE. Yeah, right. Something that is like so remote it doesn't even register.

DONALD. But there is a chance.

ANNIE. A chance of what, Donald?

DONALD. A chance that Elliot could make you happier than you could ever imagine and therefore, turn out to be your Mr. Right?

ANNIE. Get real.

DONALD. You're the one who said you knew for sure and then you went and did this. *(Donald puts his fingers an inch apart.)*

ANNIE. All right, fine. I don't know for sure, okay? No one can know that.

DONALD. I did.

ANNIE. Oh, you did.

DONALD. Yes.

ANNIE. You knew.

DONALD. That's right.

ANNIE. I see. What was it? Love at first sight across a crowded room, music playing, birds singing, something like that?

DONALD. Something like that.

ANNIE. You didn't know. You had a feeling.

DONALD. I knew I had a lot of feelings all of which reinforced what I already knew. She was the one who didn't know. In fact, she didn't have any feelings for me whatsoever. I was, what you would call, her Mr. Half Right. And that's probably padding the percentages a little bit in my favor. But, in the end, Mr. Half Right turned out to be Mr. All Right.

ANNIE. Y'know, it's nice to know I'll be living next to someone whose life is a perpetual happy ending. Be a nice juxtaposition to my own existence.

DONALD. It took a lot of lunches. And dinners. And flowers and gifts and anything else I could think of until finally, at long last, she gave me the one thing I wanted.

ANNIE. Which was?

31

DONALD. A chance. And once I had that, she was as good as mine. *(Lights change. Italian music. Elliot comes in, wearing a tie and sports jacket. A valiant attempt to look nice on no budget. Donald seats Elliot in Donald's vacated seat. Annie and Elliot at Piccolo's.)*

ELLIOT. Sorry. There was a line, can you believe it?

ANNIE. I learned long ago to count the women in the restaurant. If there's one at every table, make a run for it whether you have to go or not.

ELLIOT. I'll have to remember that. What's good here? Anything?

ANNIE. I hear the pasta is safe.

ELLIOT. "Eat at Piccolo's. We serve safe food." I like it already. *(Annie and Elliot study their menus. Donald watches from off to the side.)* What are you having?

ANNIE. I have no idea. *(Elliot shuts his menu.)*

ELLIOT. I feel like eggs.

ANNIE. What?

ELLIOT. I'm in the mood for some eggs. You want some eggs?

ANNIE. It's lunch.

ELLIOT. I know, but sometimes you gotta have what you gotta have. Where's a waiter?

ANNIE. Elliot, why can't you just choose something from the menu. They have fish, pasta, sandwiches — *(Annie turns to Donald.)* — eggs. He had eggs. He ordered scrambled eggs at one-thirty in the afternoon.

DONALD. Sounds like a man who knows what he wants.

ANNIE. Oh, he knew what he wanted.

ELLIOT. I have something to ask you. It's very important. And I don't want you to take this the wrong way.

ANNIE. What?

ELLIOT. Forget it.

ANNIE. What?

ELLIOT. No, never mind. I shouldn't even have brought it up.

ANNIE. Elliot.

ELLIOT. Okay, what the hell. If this goes well. Y'know. This.

ANNIE. This what?

ELLIOT. This.

ANNIE. This lunch?

32

ELLIOT. Right. If this lunch goes well and I think, so far so good, what do you think the chances are of maybe having dinner?

ANNIE. Tonight?

ELLIOT. No! Not tonight! Yeah, right. Let's have dinner tonight, we haven't even had lunch yet. No, that would be pushing it.

ANNIE. Yeah.

ELLIOT. No, I'm thinkin of, y'know, some other time. Some other night other than tonight.

ANNIE. Right.

ELLIOT. Like tomorrow night.

ANNIE. Elliot.

ELLIOT. It doesn't have to be tomorrow night. It can be not tonight and definitely not tomorrow night. It could be this weekend. It could — *(Annie turns to Donald, over Elliot who continues.)*

DONALD. He was nervous.

ANNIE. He was having a nervous breakdown. There's a difference.

ELLIOT. — be Saturday. Saturday's good for me. But if it's not good for you, we can do a Sunday brunch thing. I don't care, it's up to you, it doesn't matter to me.

ANNIE. Elliot.

ELLIOT. Yes.

ANNIE. Let's just have lunch, okay?

ELLIOT. I'm blowing it, aren't I?

ANNIE. You're not blowing anything.

ELLIOT. Yes, I am.

ANNIE. No, you're not. It's fine. Everything is fine. We're having lunch, you're about to eat some eggs, everything is fine.

ELLIOT. Okay.

ANNIE. Okay. *(To Donald.)* And then he did something that completely blew my mind.

DONALD. What?

ANNIE. Well, under normal circumstances, I wouldn't have reacted like I did. I just, I don't know, I wasn't prepared.

DONALD. For what? *(Annie turns to Elliot who picks up a breadstick and subtly "crosses" himself. Annie turns back to Donald.)*

ANNIE. *(Whisper.)* Catholic!

33

DONALD. *(Whispers back.)* So?

ANNIE. He was trying to sneak it past me, but I caught him. Usually, they're much bigger with it, y'know? They're over here and up here, they're all over the place and they don't care who sees it! But this was definitely the "I'm out in public, I don't want anyone to know I am, but I still have to do it or I'll burn in hell" version.

DONALD. So he's Catholic? So what?

ANNIE. If I'd have been smart, I'd have said, "Look, this was a bad idea. Let's just go back to the station and everybody lives happily ever after." But no, not me.

DONALD. Simply because he's Catholic?

ANNIE. No, because it came up in conversation.

DONALD. What did?

ANNIE. His being Catholic.

DONALD. Why? What did you say?

ANNIE. I didn't say anything. It was him. He's the one who said it. *(Elliot turns to Annie.)*

ELLIOT. I'm Catholic. *(Annie looks at Donald.)*

DONALD. Maybe he was just trying to make conversation.

ANNIE. Well, that's what I thought. I'm thinking okay, he's nervous, he's already spent an unusual amount of time in the men's room doing God knows what, he's just lobbied unsuccessfully for dinner and now, to keep things moving forward, he decides to come out of the closet about his religious convictions. Just making conversation. *(Elliot repeats the identical moment.)*

ELLIOT. I'm Catholic.

DONALD. I still don't see why that's such a disaster.

ANNIE. You don't say something like that to someone over lunch. If you're going to make an announcement like that, if you're going to reveal intimate details about yourself that —

DONALD. What did you say?

ANNIE. — in hindsight, would have been nice for the person who's hearing it to have, perhaps, known it was coming ahead of time, you should by all means, y'know ...

DONALD. Send up a flare?

ANNIE. Send up a flare! Exactly! It's common luncheon courtesy!

DONALD.   So what did you say? *(Annie hangs her head.)* Annie? *(Elliot repeats the identical moment.)*

ELLIOT.   I'm Catholic.

ANNIE.   Oh. Well, in that case, you should probably know I don't believe in God. *(Elliot sits there, stunned. Annie turns to Donald.)* It just came out. I didn't plan it. I didn't even know I felt that way. I'd never thought about it really. That's not true. I've thought about it a lot. I'd just never said it. Out loud. I don't believe in God.

DONALD.   It's all right.

ANNIE.   Yeah, it's all right. Everything's all right. Hey, like it matters what I think, right? … Right?

DONALD.   Right.

ANNIE.   Tell him that.

ELLIOT.   You what?

ANNIE.   I'd ask if you do, but that would be a stupid question, wouldn't it?

ELLIOT.   I don't believe this.

ANNIE.   Yeah well, that makes two of us.

ELLIOT.   Why?

ANNIE.   Why what?

ELLIOT.   Why don't you believe in God?

ANNIE.   Because I don't.

ELLIOT.   I'm … I'm stunned.

ANNIE.   Well, you're the one who wanted to go to lunch.

ELLIOT.   I know, but I didn't know you were …

ANNIE.   "I'm Catholic?" What did you expect me to say?

ELLIOT.   Lent.

ANNIE.   Lent?

ELLIOT.   It's Lent. I'm giving up pasta for Lent. That's why I ordered the eggs. That's why I told you I was Catholic.

ANNIE.   Oh. I thought you were just making conversation.

ELLIOT.   Just making conversation?

ANNIE.   Well, how was I supposed to know?

ELLIOT.   This is a lunch! We're having lunch! You don't —

ANNIE.   I know that.

ELLIOT.   — talk about the existence of God over lunch!

ANNIE.   Well fine, let's talk about something else. I don't care.

ELLIOT. We can't talk about something else! Not now!

ANNIE. Fine! So let's talk about it! *(Pause.)*

ELLIOT. So. You're an atheist.

ANNIE. No, I'm not.

DONALD. Liar.

ANNIE. *(To Donald.)* I'm not!

ELLIOT. You just said you didn't believe in God.

ANNIE. I don't not believe. I'm willing to believe. I just need, y'know, a little bit more, I don't know …

ELLIOT. Proof?

ANNIE. Proof. Yes. Proof would be nice.

ELLIOT. Like what, some miracle? Maybe the Second Coming? Would the Second Coming do it for you?

ANNIE. You can lose the attitude, Elliot. You're the one who wanted to talk religion.

ELLIOT. I'm sorry, I'm just … I'm completely at a loss here.

ANNIE. Yeah well, get in line.

ELLIOT. What about something smaller?

ANNIE. Something smaller than the Second Coming?

ELLIOT. Y'know, some everyday thing we take for granted that's inexplicable, that can't be accounted for but could be construed as a miracle.

ANNIE. I don't believe in miracles.

ELLIOT. You don't believe in …

ANNIE. I believe if we ever see a waiter that would be a miracle. How's that? Is that acceptable? Can we get off of me now?

ELLIOT. Fine.

ANNIE. Fine! *(Pause.)* What about you?

ELLIOT. What about me?

ANNIE. Why do you believe in God?

ELLIOT. I'm Catholic.

ANNIE. Yes, I know. But why do you believe?

ELLIOT. No, that's why.

ANNIE. That's why you believe?

ELLIOT. Yes.

ANNIE. Okay. But even though you're Catholic, you've had doubts.

ELLIOT. About what?

36

ANNIE. About the possibility of a Godless existence?

ELLIOT. Never.

DONALD. Liar.

ANNIE. You've always believed there was a God.

ELLIOT. Absolutely.

ANNIE. Based on what?

ELLIOT. Based on the fact that I'm Catholic.

ANNIE. That's not a reason.

ELLIOT. It's a good enough reason for me.

ANNIE. Elliot, that's like saying you believe in chocolate because there's a Hershey's plant in Pennsylvania.

ELLIOT. There is a Hershey's plant in Pennsylvania.

ANNIE. You're missing the point.

ELLIOT. There's also such a thing as chocolate.

ANNIE. Fine. Look. Forget you're Catholic for a second.

ELLIOT. Forget I'm Catholic?

ANNIE. Yes.

ELLIOT. I can't forget I'm Catholic. It's ingrained, imbedded —

ANNIE. Just try.

ELLIOT. — it's tattooed on my soul.

ANNIE. Why do you, Elliot Brown, the person, the individual, the human being, believe without a doubt, no questions asked, one hundred percent guaranteed, that there is a God?

ELLIOT. Listen, if you'd gotten whacked on the back of the head by Sister Mary Bernice as many times as I did, you'd believe there was a God, too.

ANNIE. So you believe out of fear.

ELLIOT. It wasn't fear.

ANNIE. A woman dressed in black beat you in the name of the Father, Son and Holy Ghost, Elliot. Don't tell me it wasn't fear.

ELLIOT. Okay, technically, there was some fear.

ANNIE. And out of that fear, you never once thought there might not be a God?

ELLIOT. No.

ANNIE. Not once.

ELLIOT. Never. Never crossed my mind. It's not even crossing my mind now.

ANNIE. Carl Sagan? Stephen Hawking? Ever heard them talk

about God?

ELLIOT. Carl Sagan and —

ANNIE. The answer is —

ELLIOT. — Stephen Hawking?

ANNIE. — no, you haven't because they don't. They avoid the subject completely.

ELLIOT. Just because they don't talk about it —

ANNIE. And what about NASA?

ELLIOT. NASA? What's NASA got to do with —

ANNIE. All those satellites and nuclear-powered telescopes on all those California mountain tops pointed towards the heavens, beaming back pictures from every corner of the galaxy and nowhere, not in one photograph that's come back has there ever been anything remotely resembling something that could possibly pass for God?

ELLIOT. I think you're putting far too much faith in a federal agency.

ANNIE. Am I?

ELLIOT. Yes.

ANNIE. You don't think they want to find it?

ELLIOT. I don't have faintest idea what they want.

ANNIE. Okay then. What about Houdini?

ELLIOT. The magician?

ANNIE. He made a pledge.

ELLIOT. To the station?

ANNIE. No. He's dead. Houdini's been —

ELLIOT. That's what —

ANNIE. — dead for year.

ELLIOT. — I thought, that's why I, y'know.

ANNIE. True story. On his deathbed, Houdini made this promise. One last trick, as it were. He told his wife that one year after he died, on the following Halloween night, he wanted her to gather all of his closest friends right there in that very same room and hold a seance. And during that seance, if there truly were an afterlife, a heaven, a God of any kind, he would come to them. Proving it was so. Well, guess what? They're still waiting.

ELLIOT. That doesn't prove anything.

ANNIE. No, but it doesn't help, does it?

ELLIOT.   Maybe God wasn't a big Houdini fan.

ANNIE.   All right, then what about this? Tell me why Jesus was born.

ELLIOT.   Why?

ANNIE.   Yes, and don't go off on the Immaculate Conception because I don't even want to get into that. All I want to know is why you think he was born.

ELLIOT.   Because God so loved the world he gave —

ANNIE.   Don't quote the Bible. I don't want the Bible. I'm asking you. Why do you, Elliot, think Jesus was brought into this world?

ELLIOT.   To bring the message of God to the people.

ANNIE.   Why?

ELLIOT.   To spread the word of God.

ANNIE.   Why?

ELLIOT.   Because they needed to hear it.

ANNIE.   Because why?

ELLIOT.   Because they were a bunch of fuck-ups! *(Elliot whips his head around to see if anyone overheard him.)*

ANNIE.   Exactly! Okay. The whole world was full of fuck ups. Everywhere you looked there was chaos. Tyranny, genocide, starvation, disease, power, greed, corruption, wars, no morals, no values, no sense of right and wrong — they were barbaric times, right?

ELLIOT.   Right.

ANNIE.   So God sent Jesus to show them the way.

ELLIOT.   Yes.

ANNIE.   So what's changed? Two thousand years later and what's different? Except for technology, everywhere you look it's still the same as it was then. I turn on the evening news and I watch a three-year-old Bosnian girl, nude from the waist down, shitting herself to death in the mud and snow. I listen to yet another team of investigators tell me about another black box discovered in yet another airplane that blew up all in the name of somebody's idea of religion.

ELLIOT.   Religion is —

ANNIE.   I watch live reports about death from Oklahoma City,

Atlanta, Beirut, Belfast, Sarajevo, Kosovo, Somalia, Romania, Tiananmen Square, Chechnya, Jerusalem — Jerusalem! Forty five kids are gunned down in a San Diego McDonald's. Two days later it's Texas. Five years later it's Columbine. Pick a city. Pick a town. Pick the place where somebody'll snap next week.

ELLIOT. Annie.

ANNIE. AIDS, leukemia, cancer, racism, fascism, sexism. If you're poor, you're lazy. If you're raped, you asked for it. Hatred overwhelms love. Greed wins out over compassion and meanwhile, our own Christian based government is either going to war or sponsoring one, not to fight for freedom but because it's good for business because there's lots of money to be made when other people die, by God. And to comfort us, all we have to soothe us, to make everything okay again is an 800 number we can call to talk to someone —

ELLIOT. That's not even fair —

ANNIE. — who will pray for us in Jesus' name so long as we support the right political party! That's why I wonder. That's why I question whether there truly is a God. Because if He came then, why isn't He coming now? *(Pause.)*

ELLIOT. If He came back now, it would mean we failed. We didn't learn anything.

ANNIE. Well, maybe we know too much.

ELLIOT. Maybe. And maybe we don't know as much as we think. Besides, it would be too late.

ANNIE. Too late for what?

ELLIOT. For you.

ANNIE. For me?

ELLIOT. There's no use saying you believe in Him after He's come back, after —

ANNIE. I don't believe in Him, Elliot.

ELLIOT. — He's, I know —

ANNIE. Today. Tomorrow. Ever.

ELLIOT. — I know, you told me, you told me already. But, y'know, all I'm saying is, what if you're wrong? *(Off Annie's reaction.)* No, what if you're wrong and He does come back? Or something happens that tells you? Y'know, provides proof? *(Donald sketches.)*

DONALD.   Being in the right place at the right time.

ELLIOT.   That shows us that this whole natural universe we thought we knew is merely a step to something else. Something so beautiful, it's inconceivable.

DONALD.   Love at first sight.

ELLIOT.   So beyond what we think we know to be true.

DONALD.   Finding something you thought was lost forever.

ELLIOT.   Something maybe we aren't supposed to understand.

ANNIE.   *(To Donald.)* Lost what?

DONALD.   I'm just thinking. Maybe Houdini had the right idea, but just went about it in the wrong way.

ANNIE.   Are you Catholic, too?

DONALD.   No. I prefer to put my money into mutual funds.

ANNIE.   But you believe in God.

DONALD.   I believe there is no way on earth I possess that talent necessary to paint my wife that day. But I did.

ANNIE.   Maybe it was Houdini.

DONALD.   Yes. Maybe it was Houdini. *(Donald holds Annie with a look.)*

ELLIOT.   What if you're right? What if Houdini had come back and proved you were right? "I've come back and I'm here to tell you, there is no afterlife. There's no God. There's no heaven. There's nothing. Jesus Christ was just a carpenter's son with a lot of good ideas." Would you really want to know that?

DONALD.   Would you?

ANNIE.   I don't know what I want to know anymore.

ELLIOT.   I lied.

ANNIE.   What?

ELLIOT.   *(Unemotional.)* When I told you I never had doubts. I have. True story. Both my parents died when I was young. My father went first. My mother lasted until I was fifteen. Cancer. Boom, she had it. Boom, she was gone. There was almost no time to take it in. My brother and I went to live with my grandparents. Very Catholic. Which was good because we were kind of lost. Alone, except for each other. And I remember thinking, where did she go? The priest told me she was in heaven because God needed her, and I remember telling him, "Yeah, but I need her more." And that was the first time I thought that maybe there wasn't any

41

heaven. Or a God. At least one I would want to be with. I mean, He took my mother away from me. And I told my brother and he said he didn't believe in heaven anymore either, but that he still believed in angels. And mom was an angel. That way she could still be alive. At least in his head. And I said, "Yeah, but if there's no heaven, where do the angels go? Do they just fly around forever or what?" And we didn't really have an answer for that. Anyway, we turned out okay, the both of us. He's down in Fort Wayne now, running his own supermarket. Wife, four kids, house, y'know. And then about two years ago, I was asleep one night and I had this dream where I saw her. I saw my mom. She sat right on the edge of my bed, looking at me. And I sat up. Hugged her. And I could feel her. I could actually smell her. And then she talked to me. Asked me how I was doing. If I was okay. And I told her I was fine but that I missed her and she said she missed me, too, and that she was glad I hadn't forgotten her. And then I woke up. And I sat there in the middle of the night, bawling my eyes out because I could still smell her. Feel her. Few weeks later, I saw my brother. Told him about it. And he said, "Oh, my God," and started crying. And I said, "What? What is it?" and he said, "I had the same exact dream two weeks ago." ... Now, I don't know if that proves anything. But it happened. Weird, huh?

ANNIE.   I'm the one who's weird.

ELLIOT.   No, you're not.

DONALD.   Yes, she is.

ELLIOT.   You're just looking for answers just like everybody else. You just haven't found any you like yet. Let me ask you this. If you don't believe there's a God up in heaven, what about down here? Do you believe in heaven on earth?

ANNIE.   Donald does.

ELLIOT.   Donald? Who's Donald?

ANNIE.   He's just this guy.

DONALD.   Just this guy?

ANNIE.   Lives across the hall from me. He has this wife he adores. It borders on the maniacally romantic.

DONALD.   Thanks a lot.

ANNIE.   Well, it does. I'm sorry.

DONALD.   I think I liked you better when you lied to me.

ANNIE. You'll like this next part. *(To Elliot.)* The thing is for Donald, she is heaven. His heaven. You should see the way he lights up whenever he talks about her. It's as if nothing else exists. His whole world begins and ends with her. Can you imagine being that in love with someone? *(Elliot stares at Annie. Annie turns away towards Donald, realizing.)* Oh, God.

DONALD. Did he answer you?

ANNIE. Oh, yeah. *(Annie and Donald turn to Elliot, who continues to gaze at Annie.)*

ELLIOT. Yes. Yes, I can.

ANNIE. *(Staring at Elliot.)* Donald?

DONALD. It's all right. *(Annie reaches across the table and kisses Elliot. .The lights fade down first on Annie and Elliot and then on Donald who stands there, smiling.)*

END OF ACT ONE

ACT TWO

Lights up on Elliot's apartment. Some of Elliot and Annie's clothes are strewn about the floor.

Annie stands, looking out the downstage window. Elliot enters quietly. Elliot picks up her sweater, smells it and goes to her.

ELLIOT. There you are. I wondered where you went.

ANNIE. I'm right here.

ELLIOT. I didn't see you go out.

ANNIE. I was just admiring your view. It's a lot better than mine.

ELLIOT. It's a parking lot.

ANNIE. Yeah well, like I said. We should be getting back.

ELLIOT. Yeah, we should get going. *(Neither of them moves.)*

ANNIE. Are you all right?

ELLIOT. Me? I'm fine.

ANNIE. I mean, physically.

ELLIOT. Physically?

ANNIE. Are you physically all right?

ELLIOT. Yes. Why?

ANNIE. I thought I hurt you.

ELLIOT. No, not at all.

ANNIE. You're sure?

ELLIOT. Positive. You just took me by surprise is all.

ANNIE. I'm sorry.

ELLIOT. No, don't be sorry. Please. *(Elliot reaches up to touch Annie's hair.)* It was incredible. *(Elliot turns away, wincing in pain.)*

ANNIE. What's wrong with your shoulder?

ELLIOT. Nothing.

ANNIE. It's broken, isn't it?

44

ELLIOT.   It just popped out, but it popped right back in. Really. It happens all the time.

ANNIE.   I separated your shoulder?

ELLIOT.   No.

ANNIE.   I separated your shoulder.

ELLIOT.   You did not separate my shoulder.

ANNIE.   I knew it. *(Annie takes Elliot's hand. Elliot twists to the floor in pain.)*

ELLIOT.   Annie!

ANNIE.   I'm sorry, I'm sorry! God, I knew it as soon as we rolled off the bed.

ELLIOT.   That was my knee.

ANNIE.   What?

ELLIOT.   When we rolled off the bed, my knee went out. My shoulder popped out when we slammed into the headboard.

ANNIE.   Oh, God.

ELLIOT.   But when you wrapped your legs around my neck and squeezed …

ANNIE.   I didn't mean to squeeze that hard.

ELLIOT.   No, I'm not complaining. Really, it's okay. Once I got my air passage clear, I was fine.

ANNIE.   I'm sorry, Elliot. I don't know what got into me.

ELLIOT.   Are you kidding me? You blew Kathy Callihan right out of the water.

ANNIE.   Kathy who?

ELLIOT.   The night of my Senior Prom. Until today, the single greatest sexual experience of my life.

ANNIE.   I don't think I want to hear this.

ELLIOT.   No, it's a good thing. All the motels were booked solid. We couldn't get a room to save our lives. And she wanted it to be special, y'know? What with it being the Prom and all so that meant the back seat was out so I had to come up with something fast. And then I realized we were both Catholic and I remembered from my days as an altar boy that Father Harvey always left the doors to the church unlocked, y'know, in case some insomniac needed to pray in the middle of the night or something. So we decided to go there.

ANNIE.   To a church?

45

ELLIOT. Yeah.

ANNIE. You did it in a church?

ELLIOT. In a Catholic church.

ANNIE. You did it inside the church?

ELLIOT. It wasn't like we did it in the middle of Easter Mass. There was nobody there, we were —

ANNIE. I can't —

ELLIOT. — by ourselves.

ANNIE. — believe this. Where did you do it?

ELLIOT. Well, Callahan wanted to do it up on the altar. She grabbed my hand and said, "C'mon, Elliot. We're about to get as close to God as two people can possibly get."

ANNIE. Up on the…?

ELLIOT. Trust me, it didn't happen. I said, "Callahan, we can't do it up on the altar. That would be sacrilegious. Let's do it in a pew." Lucky for me, she said yes. How about you?

ANNIE. I didn't go to my Senior Prom.

ELLIOT. No. I meant, how does this afternoon rank with you?

ANNIE. Rank?

ELLIOT. Yeah.

ANNIE. I don't rank things like this, Elliot.

ELLIOT. Just give me a number. Scale of one to ten. Ten being the best, one being the worst.

ANNIE. I'm not going to assign some number —

ELLIOT. For me, it was a thirty-seven. Maybe a thirty-eight.

ANNIE. Elliot.

ELLIOT. Please. One through ten. *(Pause.)*

ANNIE. Ten. *(Annie gets up and goes out. Elliot glows.)* You should get some ice on that shoulder. Do you have an ice bag?

ELLIOT. Under the sink. Annie?

ANNIE. *(O.S.)* I'm listening.

ELLIOT. Was there anything I did in particular that, y'know, caused that ten? Y'know, some move, some technique, anything. And before you say it, I know I didn't do anything that came close to your legs around the neck, triple axle, double twist, scissor kick. But if there was anything that, y'know … *(Pause.)* Anything. *(Pause.)* Anything at all. *(Donald enters. A combination of Elliot and Annie's apartments.)*

46

DONALD. Why didn't you answer him?

ANNIE. *(O.S.)* I did answer him.

DONALD. And?

ANNIE. *(O.S.)* You don't want to know.

DONALD. Of course I do.

ANNIE. *(O.S.)* No, you don't.

DONALD. Why wouldn't I want to know? *(Both Donald and Elliot are looking off at Annie.)*

ANNIE. *(O.S.)* I told him the truth.

DONALD. About what?

ANNIE. *(O.S.)* About everything.

DONALD. Well, that's good.

ANNIE. *(O.S.)* No, that's not good. I'd have been better off lying to his face.

DONALD. Why? Was the sex that bad?

ANNIE. *(O.S.)* No, the sex was like the greatest sex in the history of human beings.

DONALD. So why would you possibly want to lie to him? *(Annie enters with a blue ice bag.)*

ANNIE. Because he had nothing to do with it.

DONALD. What are you talking about, he had nothing to do with it? He was there, wasn't he?

ANNIE. Yes, but he wasn't the only one.

DONALD. There were more than…? You had a menage a trois?

ANNIE. I don't want to talk about it.

DONALD. Wait a minute. I do. I want to talk about it.

ELLIOT. Anything. Anything at all.

DONALD. Who else was involved here?

ELLIOT. At least tell me I was in the room.

DONALD. Annie?

ANNIE. All right, fine. *(To Elliot.)* There was one thing.

ELLIOT. Thank God. What? What was it?

ANNIE. Did you growl?

ELLIOT. Did I…?

ANNIE. Did you growl? I heard a growl.

ELLIOT. A growl.

ANNIE. Yes. You don't have a dog, do you?

ELLIOT. A dog?

ANNIE. You don't own a dog.

ELLIOT. They don't allow pets in the building.

DONALD. You heard a growl?

ANNIE. *(To Donald.)* Can I tell the story?

DONALD. Sorry.

ANNIE. It was right when I, y'know, when my legs wrapped around your ...

ELLIOT. Neck?

ANNIE. Right. That's when I heard it.

ELLIOT. That's when you heard the ...

ANNIE. Yes.

ELLIOT. Did that please you?

ANNIE. So you're admitting it?

ELLIOT. Not necessarily.

ANNIE. What's that supposed to mean?

ELLIOT. I don't know.

ANNIE. Did you growl, Elliot?

ELLIOT. Maybe.

ANNIE. You either growled or you didn't. There's no halfway on this one.

ELLIOT. I understand.

ANNIE. While we were having sex, did you growl? Yes or no. *(Pause.)*

ELLIOT. Remember that documentary on the mating habits of the Siberian Polar Bear?

ANNIE. Oh, God.

ELLIOT. I think that may have connected with me on some deep, subconscious level.

ANNIE. Oh, God.

DONALD. This is starting to get interesting.

ANNIE. You had a bear fantasy?

ELLIOT. No.

ANNIE. You had a bear fantasy.

ELLIOT. No, I didn't.

ANNIE. You thought you were a bear.

ELLIOT. I did not think I was a bear.

ANNIE. You thought I was a bear?

48

ELLIOT. I didn't think anybody was a bear!

DONALD. What's wrong with being a bear?

ANNIE. I don't believe this.

ELLIOT. I was simply reacting to what you were doing.

ANNIE. You didn't hear me growl, did you? Did you hear me growl, Elliot?

ELLIOT. No, I didn't —

ANNIE. So, if you —

ELLIOT. — hear you growl.

ANNIE. — didn't hear me growl, how could you possibly be reacting to me?

ELLIOT. You did one of her moves.

ANNIE. One of whose moves?

ELLIOT. The female bear. In *A Siberian Love Affair*. At least I thought you did.

ANNIE. What?

ELLIOT. When you wrapped your legs around my neck. She does the same exact thing in the documentary. The only difference is when she did it, she growled. Which is what threw me because I thought you were doing what she did, which don't get me wrong, I didn't mind at all but when you didn't growl I thought that meant you wanted me to, so I did. I growled.

ANNIE. You thought I was using the sexual technique of a polar bear?

ELLIOT. It's not like that.

ANNIE. I didn't get that particular move from a bear, okay? Trust me on this one.

ELLIOT. Well, wherever you got it, it worked. For both of us. Didn't it? *(Nothing from Annie.)* It worked for both of us, didn't it, Annie? When you wrapped your legs around my neck and I growled it was at that moment, that very moment, we were beyond anything I'd ever experienced. We were primal. We were pure, Annie. There was this connection, this bridge, this link between us, the bears, the whole universe. It was as if our bodies made way for our souls and they came together at that very moment and when they did, I swear it was like a shot of whiskey times a thousand. That's what I felt. Is that what you felt? Annie? ... Annie?

49

DONALD. Annie?

ANNIE. Yes.

ELLIOT. I knew it! I knew it! Wait a minute. Are you saying, is that when you ... I mean, did you, y'know. Y'know.

ANNIE. Did I what?

ELLIOT. Y'know.

ANNIE. Come?

ELLIOT. Right then?

ANNIE. Yes.

ELLIOT. You ... you ...

ANNIE. Came.

ELLIOT. Right then?

ANNIE. Yes.

ELLIOT. Oh, God.

ANNIE. Elliot?

ELLIOT. I did, too. At the same time. Right then. I did, too.

ANNIE. I know.

ELLIOT. Oh, my God! Do you know what this means? Do you know how rare it is for two people who've never been together before in their lives to, y'know ...

ANNIE. Come.

ELLIOT. At the same time?

ANNIE. Well, I have a confession to make.

ELLIOT. What?

ANNIE. I had more than one.

DONALD. You what?

ANNIE. *(To Donald.)* Why am I telling you this?

DONALD. I don't know, but whatever you do, don't stop now.

ELLIOT. Wait a minute. Are you saying, are you saying you had multiple ...

ANNIE. Yes.

ELLIOT. *(To heaven.)* Thank you, Jesus!

ANNIE. Actually, I had more than I could count. Not that I was counting. Which I was for awhile, until I lost count.

ELLIOT. You were counting your ...

ANNIE. Orgasms, yes. Don't ask me why. For some reason, I just found myself wanting to keep some sort of tally of what was happening to me, I guess, I don't know.

ELLIOT. *(To himself.)* God, why don't I keep a diary? It doesn't matter, I'll start one today.

DONALD. You were counting your...?

ANNIE. I stopped at eight.

DONALD. Eight?

ANNIE. It might've been nine. Maybe ten. I'm not sure.

ELLIOT. Ten?

DONALD. Ten?

ANNIE. At least.

ELLIOT. You hit double figures?

DONALD. Is that humanly possible?

ANNIE. Well apparently, it is. Though Elliot thought it was something else entirely.

ELLIOT. It's a miracle.

ANNIE. What?

ELLIOT. This is a miracle. Don't you see, Annie? Don't you see what this is? God is speaking to you.

ANNIE. What are you talking about?

ELLIOT. Okay, it's a reach, I know. But it makes sense. It makes perfect sense.

ANNIE. Elliot, please.

ELLIOT. This wasn't supposed to happen, Annie. It really wasn't. You, me, this. But then, all of a sudden for some inexplicable reason, it all fell into place. You and Richard break up, we go to lunch, we talk about God, God listens, we come back —

ANNIE. God listens?

ELLIOT. — to my place, we do the Siberian Shuffle, you hit double figures — it's a gift from God!

ANNIE. A gift from God?

ELLIOT. It has to be! It can't possibly be anything else! Don't you see? He's answering our prayers.

ANNIE. I don't pray, Elliot.

ELLIOT. My prayers then! He's answering my prayers! And believe me, I've been praying for this for years!

ANNIE. This was not a gift from God, Elliot.

ELLIOT. You don't know that.

ANNIE. Oh, I'm pretty damn sure.

51

ELLIOT. Okay, fine. I don't know that it is, you don't know that it isn't. But don't you just love the idea that it might be? Wouldn't it be just the greatest thing ever if somehow we could prove to you God had a hand in this?

ANNIE. Something tells me the hand of God doesn't work this way.

ELLIOT. Let's call in sick.

ANNIE. What?

ELLIOT. I'm going to call the station and tell Larry.

ANNIE. Elliot, no!

ELLIOT. What'll I tell him? I know! We ate some bad shellfish!

ANNIE. We can't call in sick. We're in the middle of a pledge drive.

ELLIOT. So Big Bird dies, so what? He's just a bird. Pull the plug.

ANNIE. Elliot!

ELLIOT. Annie, I can't prove it. But what if we went back in there and did it again and the same exact thing happened? What would it mean?

ANNIE. It would mean you'd have two separated shoulders.

ELLIOT. It would mean God is speaking to us.

ANNIE. God didn't speak to us, Elliot.

ELLIOT. This could change the Catholic Church as we know it. At least as I know it.

ANNIE. Tell you what, I'm going to save us both. I'll meet you down in the — *(Elliot grabs Annie and kisses her passionately. Annie kisses him back. Donald strolls over.)*

DONALD. Let's go back in there so God can speak to us again? *(Annie tries to talk to Donald through Elliot's kiss.)*

ANNIE. Mmm-mmmm …

DONALD. That just might be the greatest religiously inspired pick up line since Adam offered Eve a rib.

ANNIE. Mm-mmmm …

DONALD. Y'know, even a blind man could see he's in love with you. It's just a question of when you decide you're ready to fall in love with him.

ANNIE. *(No.)* Mm-mmmm …

DONALD. Yes, you will. *(Annie breaks out of the kiss. Elliot starts kissing his way down Annie's body while Annie talks to Donald.)*

ANNIE.   Elliot is Elliot. He will always be Elliot and as long as he's Elliot, I don't see falling in love as an option.

DONALD.   You don't know that.

ANNIE.   Okay, fine. I don't know it, but I would assume I would at least feel something.

ELLIOT.   Grrr ...

ANNIE.   One! *(Annie turns and falls into Elliot as they both sink to the floor. Elliot grabs both of Annie's breasts from behind.)*

DONALD.   It sounds as if you felt plenty.

ANNIE.   For him. Felt something for him.

ELLIOT.   Grrr ...

ANNIE.   Two! *(Annie turns around, faces Elliot and climbs him, her feet standing on his thighs. Elliot lifts her skirt. His head disappears.)*

DONALD.   Well, what is it you think you're not feeling?

ANNIE.   I don't know.

DONALD.   He's certainly passionate.

ANNIE.   He's very passionate, yes — *(Annie turns to Donald and is instantly lucid, all the while Elliot continues to groan from somewhere under Annie's skirt.)* — but then he's in public broadcasting. I mean, you can't do what we do and not be passionate about it. It's part of the job description. *(Annie's body tenses as her feet lift off Elliot's thighs. Her entire weight is now balanced on his upturned face.)*

ELLIOT.   Grrr!

ANNIE.   Three!

ELLIOT.   Grrr!

ANNIE.   Four!

ELLIOT.   Grrr!

ANNIE.   Five!

DONALD.   Passion is what makes you feel truly alive.

ANNIE.   Yes, but it can also get in the way. Two overly — *(Annie falls over onto Elliot's back, talking to Donald from over Elliot's ass.)* — passionate people are like a train wreck waiting to happen —

ELLIOT.   Grrr!

ANNIE.   — Six! Listen, if you can prove God had something to do with what happened this afternoon, I'll be more than happy to fall in love with Elliot. But until that happens, it was just a nice afternoon —

ELLIOT. Grrr!

ANNIE. Seven!

ELLIOT. Grrr!

ANNIE. — with a fellow employee —

ELLIOT. Grrr! *(Annie slaps Elliot on the ass.)*

ANNIE. — Eight! Who growled like a bear and when he did, I saw ...

DONALD. You saw what?

ANNIE. Oh, God.

ELLIOT. Grrr! *(Annie slaps Elliot's ass again.)*

ANNIE. Nine! Nine! Nine! I saw ...

DONALD. What?

ANNIE. I saw ...

DONALD. What? You saw what?

ANNIE. You!

DONALD. Me?

ANNIE. *(With Elliot.)* Donald! *(Everything stops. Elliot falls flat onto the floor. Annie stares at Donald. Pause.)* I saw you. Right in front of me. More real than you are now.

ELLIOT. *(From under Annie's skirt.)* Did you just say, "Donald"?

ANNIE. Ten. *(Annie rolls off Elliot.)*

DONALD. Oh, no.

ANNIE. Oh, God.

ELLIOT. Donald?

ANNIE. Oh, God.

DONALD. Oh, no.

ELLIOT. You said, "Donald."

ANNIE. Did I?

ELLIOT. You said, "Donald."

ANNIE. When?

DONALD. How could you see me? I wasn't there.

ELLIOT. Just now.

ANNIE. Are you sure? Maybe I growled. Maybe it was just a growl.

ELLIOT. You didn't growl. You said, "Donald." Even with your thighs in my ears, I could hear you.

ANNIE.   *(To Donald.)* It was no use. He heard it.

DONALD.   Why in the world would you —

ANNIE.   Because I saw you!

DONALD.   You saw me where?

ANNIE.   There!

DONALD.   Where?

ANNIE.   Right in front of me!

DONALD.   But I wasn't there.

ANNIE.   Oh, you were there, all right.

DONALD.   But you were with Elliot. I wasn't even in the room.

ANNIE.   Elliot was in the room, but you were the one I was with.

DONALD.   What's that supposed to mean?

ANNIE.   It means what it means, Donald. It means I was with you. Why? I don't know.

DONALD.   How was Elliot?

ELLIOT.   It's okay. I understand. These things happen.

ANNIE.   What?

ELLIOT.   Forget it.

ANNIE.   No. Wait a minute.

ELLIOT.   You didn't mean it.

ANNIE.   No, I meant it. I said it.

ELLIOT.   I know.

ANNIE.   I'm admitting it, Elliot. I'm telling you I said his name.

ELLIOT.   I know.

ANNIE.   While I was with you.

ELLIOT.   And I'm telling you, it's okay. You accidentally blurted out something that wasn't real, that didn't really happen —

ANNIE.   It happened, Elliot! I saw him! He was there, for a split second he was there and I forgot where I was!

ELLIOT.   He's just a neighbor, right?

ANNIE.   He's what?

ELLIOT.   He's just your neighbor.

ANNIE.   He's my neighbor, yes. So what? What does that have to do with anything?

ELLIOT.   Is he here now?

ANNIE.   Is he what?

ELLIOT.   Is he here now? Do you see him now?

55

ANNIE. No, of course not.

ELLIOT. So then, he's not here. But I am. And I was. And so were you. So I don't care what you think you saw or who's name pops out of your mouth, all I know is you were with me and I was with you and it was incredible and nothing is going to change that.

ANNIE. It's not that simple.

ELLIOT. It doesn't matter, Annie.

ANNIE. Yes, it does!

ELLIOT. No, it doesn't. The only one it should matter to is me and if it doesn't matter to me, it shouldn't matter to you. So let's just forget about it, all right?

ANNIE. I can't just forget about it.

ELLIOT. Yes, you can. I've forgotten about it already. As far as I'm concerned —

ANNIE. I can't just dismiss this —

ELLIOT. — it never happened.

ANNIE. — like it, I can't just dismiss this like it —

ELLIOT. It doesn't matter, it's no big deal.

ANNIE. — never even happened, Elliot! It is a big deal! It's a very big deal!

ELLIOT. Why does it have to be such a —

ANNIE. Because I might be falling in love with him! *(Pause. Donald hangs his head. Elliot is stunned.)* I didn't mean that.

ELLIOT. You might …

ANNIE. I didn't mean that. I didn't mean to say that.

ELLIOT. Are you seeing him?

ANNIE. Not right now, no.

ELLIOT. No. I meant, are you seeing him?

ANNIE. No. Of course not.

ELLIOT. But you want to.

ANNIE. I don't know. I just said it. I don't know why. I just did. I'm sorry. Look, you were wonderful, Elliot, you really were …

ELLIOT. Are you in love with him?

ANNIE. I don't know.

ELLIOT. No. You have to know. You have to know, Annie. I don't know is not acceptable. I'm not going to let you get away with I don't know anymore. You have to know. You have to. Are you in love with Donald or not? Are you in love with Donald, Annie? Yes or no. Yes or no, Annie —

ANNIE.   Yes. *(Pause. Elliot doesn't move. Annie hangs her head. Donald gets up and walks U., the sound of his footsteps the only thing we hear.)* I'm sorry.

ELLIOT.   Yeah, so am I. *(Elliot gets up.)* We should be getting back. I have to change. I'm gonna go change.

ANNIE.   I'll wait for you in the car.

ELLIOT.   I have a better idea. There's the number of a taxi service next to the phone in the kitchen? Call it. That way when I come back out, you won't be here anymore. *(Elliot goes off. Lights change. Annie's apartment.)*

ANNIE.   I'm not trying to break up your marriage, I'm really not. This probably isn't even that. It's probably something else entirely. Like salmonella poisoning or something.

DONALD.   Are you falling in love with me?

ANNIE.   God, I hope not.

DONALD.   Why do you say that?

ANNIE.   Because I don't want to, that's why.

DONALD.   Why not?

ANNIE.   Because I don't. I can't.

DONALD.   Yes, you can.

ANNIE.   You're married.

DONALD.   Yes.

ANNIE.   Happily married.

DONALD.   Very happily married. That doesn't mean I can't love you or you can't love me.

ANNIE.   Yeah right, here we go. I forgot I was talking to the Mayor of Sunshine Acres. Look, this is stupid. I should never have told you about this.

DONALD.   Yes, you should've.

ANNIE.   I don't even know you, Elliot!

DONALD.   Donald.

ANNIE.   Donald! We've known each other what, a week? This is ridiculous! And besides … never mind.

DONALD.   Don't hold back now. You're on a roll.

ANNIE.   I'm not falling in love with you. I can't be falling in love

57

with you because when I look at you, like right now, I don't find you in the least bit attractive.

DONALD. You mean, physically?

ANNIE. Physically, metaphysically. I look at you and nothing happens. I'm not tingling. I'm not longing for your touch. I'm not imagining how I couldn't possibly live without you which I would think I would be doing if I were truly falling in love with you.

DONALD. Y'know, a remark like that would kill a lesser man.

ANNIE. I'm sorry. I'm just trying to be honest.

DONALD. No, please. By all means. So you're saying there's no attraction whatsoever.

ANNIE. No.

DONALD. None?

ANNIE. No.

DONALD. Nothing at all. Not even ... *(Donald holds up two fingers an inch apart, as does Annie.)*

ANNIE. Not even.

DONALD. I see. But there must be something. I mean, you did see me.

ANNIE. There is one thing. But I don't know that it's ... I don't know.

DONALD. Tell me ... .Just tell me, Annie.

ANNIE. You make me unafraid. I tell you things I haven't even told myself. I'm drawn to that. As strongly as I was drawn to Elliot this afternoon. No, this was more than that. This was ... it was like everything was suddenly in perfect focus and all I could see was your face. And your eyes. Everything was in your eyes. And I could feel myself go into them. Towards them. And when I did, I could feel myself let go. Completely. And when I did, I was free. For the first time in maybe my whole life, I was free. Or everything. And that's when I ... started counting.

DONALD. What was I doing?

ANNIE. What?

DONALD. When you saw me. With Elliot. What was I doing?

ANNIE. You were just standing there.

DONALD. That's all?

ANNIE. You had your hand out. *(Donald extends his hand.)*

DONALD. Like this? *(The lights begin to change.)*

ANNIE. Yes. And there was —

DONALD. Music? *(Music fades up.)*

ANNIE. Yes.

DONALD. A waltz? *(A waltz can be heard. The cellist.)*

ANNIE. Yes. *(Donald goes towards Annie, his hand extended.)*

DONALD. Do you know how to waltz, Annie Wilson?

ANNIE. Yes.

DONALD. Liar.

ANNIE. No. *(Annie takes Donald's hand.)*

DONALD. You know, you haven't truly lived until you've waltzed with the one you love. *(The lights have now changed to Annie's VISION. Donald and Annie begin to waltz around the room. Unlike before, they dance beautifully, gliding together, never taking their eyes off each other. Finally, after several beats of dancing, Donald slows them down until Donald and Annie are standing with each other, holding each other, staring at each other. And then, Annie kisses Donald. Tenderly. The music ends. After a few beats, Donald breaks the kiss.)* This isn't real.

ANNIE. But I can feel you. I can touch you. I can taste you. *(The lights begin to fade back to reality.)* No. No. What's happening to me?

DONALD. Nothing's happening to you.

ANNIE. What are you doing?

DONALD. I'm not doing anything.

ANNIE. Yes, you are.

DONALD. I'm just standing here.

ANNIE. Well, stop it!

DONALD. Stop what?

ANNIE. Why are you doing this?

DONALD. Why am I doing what, Annie?

ANNIE. Why are you leading me around like this?

DONALD. I want to.

ANNIE. Why?

DONALD. Because.

ANNIE. But why? Why do you care? You don't even know me! Why do you care so much about me?

DONALD. I think it's time to call it a night.

ANNIE. Don't you dare leave me here alone. *(Annie extends her*

hand out to Donald.) Waltz with me! *(Donald stares back at Annie.)*
Waltz with me, Donald. Please. Waltz with me.

DONALD. We had a deal.

ANNIE. I know.

DONALD. You said you wouldn't.

ANNIE. I know, but I am — *(Annie grabs Donald's hands and places them in position to waltz.)* — and I can't explain it. I don't want to explain it, but I can feel it. It's real. It's so real. It's more real than anything I've ever felt in my whole life. Please. Waltz with me. I'm begging you. *(Donald is passive as they begin to waltz in place. Annie buries her face into Donald's shoulder. After a couple beats of dancing, Donald speaks quietly to Annie.)*

DONALD. My wife didn't believe in God, either. It was unfortunate because, at least for me, there's so much evidence to the contrary. I tried to convince her. She didn't want to hear it. I think she was afraid, just like you, that maybe she was right. Your life flashes before your eyes, there's nothing to hold onto. Believe in. Hope for. I tried to tell her. I said, you're missing it. We can only hope. And I for one believe, if I believe in anything, better to have some hope than no hope at all. Without hope, you aren't alive. That's what I tried to tell her over all those lunches. And dinners. But no matter how hard I tried, I couldn't convince her that what she was looking for wasn't that hard to find. I could make her happier than she could ever imagine. And then, I got a break. I somehow neglected to mention in the two years I pursued her that I had this place in the country. She said, she loved the country. So I said, how about we go away for the weekend. The only thing I ask of you is you let me paint you. I have this cottage. With this window. With this garden out back. And in the late morning, the sun will come streaming in at an angle that — and she said, yes. She agreed. On Sunday morning, the sun came out. Spring in all its glory. I couldn't mix the paint fast enough. I set up my easel. I put the old wooden chair in the window. I brought her in. Sat her down. The sun hit her just like I told her it would. I got my brush. Picked up my pallet. Took a deep breath. And just as I was about to tell her what I wanted her to do, she turned to me and said, "I love you." And that's when I knew there was a God. *(Donald breaks the embrace and looks down at Annie.)* I'm going to go now. *(Donald backs away from Annie.)*

ANNIE. I still haven't seen that painting.

DONALD. Go paint your own. *(Donald glances at the apartment before turning away and exiting through the door. Elliot enters, carrying papers and a large coffee table book. Annie's office.)*

ELLIOT. Here's the giveaway for the next break. Plus Larry's suggestions.

ANNIE. Just leave it there. I'll look at it on my way out.

ELLIOT. I think you're going to want to see this. *Two Polar Bears in the Snow: A Behind-the-Scenes Look at the Making of a Siberian Love Affair by Ulf Siederkind.* Larry thinks they'll eat it up. According to him, every time we rerun the bear show, the phones ring off the hook.

ANNIE. I'm sorry about yesterday.

ELLIOT. So am I. I overreacted.

ANNIE. No, you didn't.

ELLIOT. Yes, I did. I really did. I stopped by the church last night. Got some counseling.

ANNIE. Counseling?

ELLIOT. Yeah.

ANNIE. About what?

ELLIOT. About yesterday.

ANNIE. You talked to a priest about yesterday?

ELLIOT. No, I went over his head. I talked to God.

ANNIE. Terrific.

ELLIOT. You wanna know what He told me?

ANNIE. Not really, no.

ELLIOT. He told me to ask you to dinner tonight. He told me we should go to the same restaurant, sit at the same table, eat the same food, take the same route home —

ANNIE. Elliot.

ELLIOT. — and do the same exact thing we did and just see what happens.

ANNIE. No.

ELLIOT. What have you got to lose?

ANNIE. No, Elliot.

ELLIOT. What's the worst that can happen?

ANNIE. Stop it! No more! We had an afternoon. That's all it

61

was. One afternoon. Nothing more, nothing less.

ELLIOT.   I just thought maybe …

ANNIE.   Back off! *(Pause.)*

ELLIOT.   Okay. Okay. *(Elliot goes to Annie, grabs her face and kisses her. Annie doesn't fight him, her hands on her hips. Elliot finally breaks the kiss.)*

ANNIE.   Elliot?

ELLIOT.   You are the love of my life, Annie Wilson. I've known it since the day you stood on my desk.

ANNIE.   I can't — *(Elliot marches towards the door.)*

ELLIOT.   No, it's okay. It's all right. You do whatever it is you think you have to do with this Donald guy. But when you're done with him, and one day you will be done with him, I'll still be here. *(Elliot at the door.)* Oh, and by the way. What happened between us yesterday wasn't just an afternoon. It was a miracle. The sooner you accept it, the better. And if you were really smart, you'd fall in love with it. *(Elliot leaves, shutting the door behind him. Lights change. The TV Studio.)*

TONY.   *(Booth, intercom.)* Ten seconds. Larry wants you to remind them how if Big Bird were here, he would be the first to —

ANNIE.   I know, I know. I saw it.

TONY.   *(Booth.)* Five, four, three, two …

ANNIE.   *(To unseen camera.)* Hello and welcome back. I hope you're enjoying yet another rebroadcast of Ulf Siederkind's award-winning documentary *A Siberian Love Affair*. As a special gift for those of you who would like a momento of this wonderful film, we will send you this wonderful coffee table book of photographs taken by Ulf Siederkind himself for a donation of only one hundred dollars. I happen to have a copy right here. The book is entitled — *(Holds up book.)* — *Two Polar Bears In The Snow: A Behind The Scenes Look At The Making Of A Siberian Lover Affair By Ulf Siederkind*. I know I'm going to be wanting one in my living room and I know you will, too. So give us — *(Elliot enters, hands Annie a piece of paper, takes the coffee table book and goes out. All without looking at Annie.)* — a call right now at 1-800-555-WPBK. For those of you waiting for an update on Big Bird, we've just received a statement regarding his latest condition.

Tony, is this the latest statement regarding Big Bird's condition?

TONY. *(Booth, gravely.)* I'm afraid so, Annie.

ANNIE. This just in. *(Reading.)* "Big Bird has regained consciousness. His vital signs are stable and while his prognosis is hopeful, his chance of survival is still unknown. Doctors say that for the time being, all we can do is pray. He's in God's hands now." Liar.

(To viewers.) Not you, me. That's right, I'm lying to you. Big Bird is not sick. He is not dying. About his only concern is when he and his other friends march down Sesame Street to Wall Street and go truly public in the only sense of the word that makes any sense in this country. So, he'll be fine, no matter what happens. As I see it, about the only one who's dying here is you. And me. We walk around like ghosts. We are translucent. We don't register. We don't matter. We don't last. We have intellect, but no understanding. We love the idea of faith, but lack the· spirit to truly believe. Which is a shame because this lack of faith in even the possibility of something unfortunately makes the thought of … the thought of living … Due to certain recent events in my life, I've come to the realization that this lack of spirit, this lack of understanding is nothing more than the Faithless Person's cry for hope. Not help. Hope. I'm crying for hope. Because without it, I'm afraid … I'm afraid it's not possible for someone such as myself to believe in God. Or Big Bird. Or the universal connection between human beings and the mating habits of the Siberian Polar Bear. Y'know, I've been told by someone who knows first hand that I will not have truly lived until I've waltzed with the one I love. I don't know if he's right. But I keep listening for that music. Because I'm afraid if I never hear it, Big Bird really will die. For me. For you. For all of us. And if you let him die, you'll be taking away the one thing I have left. My soul. And that would be bad. B-A-D. Bad. *(Annie stands still for several beats. Lights change. Annie's apartment. Annie turns her head and stares at the dresser drawers. A moment of decision. Annie crosses and hurriedly begins removing clothing from the drawers. The door opens quietly. Elliot stand there with a bag of groceries.)*

ELLIOT. Annie?

ANNIE. Elliot.

ELLIOT.   I'm sorry. It was open.

ANNIE.   What are you doing here?

ELLIOT.   I was sent on behalf of everyone at the station to see if you were okay.

ANNIE.   Well, I'm okay. What's in the bag?

ELLIOT.   Eggs. *(Off Annie's look.)* I took it upon myself to pick up a few things at the corner market in the unlikely event you'd let me stay and cook you dinner.

ANNIE.   I'm sorry. I can't. I'm going out of town.

ELLIOT.   Out of town?

ANNIE.   Yes. I'm leaving tonight.

ELLIOT.   Does Larry know about this? *(Annie goes out.)*

ANNIE.   *(O.S.)* No. Could you tell him for me? I'd appreciate it.

ELLIOT.   Are you quitting the station?

ANNIE.   *(O.S.)* No, I'm just going for a — *(Annie enters with a suitcase.)* — much needed vacation, that's all.

ELLIOT.   Where are you going?

ANNIE.   Rome.

ELLIOT.   Rome?

ANNIE.   I want to see the Vatican.

ELLIOT.   The Vatican?

ANNIE.   Yes. Never been there. Dying to see it. Have you ever been?

ELLIOT.   No.

ANNIE.   And you call yourself a Catholic.

ELLIOT.   Are you going with Donald?

ANNIE.   No, Elliot. I'm not going with Donald. *(Dal appears in the door.)*

DAL.   Wide open again.

ELLIOT.   *(To Annie.)* Is this him?

ANNIE.   I'm sorry, Dal.

ELLIOT.   Are you Donald?

DAL.   Donald?

ANNIE.   No, this is Dal. He owns the building.

ELLIOT.   Oh, sorry. Elliot Brown. I'm a friend of Annie's.

ANNIE.   Elliot works with me at 68.

DAL.   Is that right?

ELLIOT.   You watch public television?

DAL. Yeah. Yeah, I do. Oh, I almost forgot. *(Dal holds out a twenty-dollar bill towards Annie.)*

ANNIE. What's this?

DAL. It's not for you. It's for your station. You're beggin' for money, aren't ya?

ANNIE. Well yeah, but ...

DAL. So take it.

ANNIE. You have to pledge it.

DAL. I'm pledgin' it right now. You want it or not?

ELLIOT. Yes, we do. Thank you.

ANNIE. Thank you, Dal.

DAL. Good. Play that bear show again.

ANNIE. What?

ELLIOT. You like that show, do you?

DAL. Me and Betty saw it the other night. We may never watch Disney again.

ANNIE. Thanks, Dal.

DAL. No problem. *(To Elliot.)* Where'd you know Mr. Peterson from?

ELLIOT. Who?

ANNIE. Donald.

ELLIOT. Oh, I don't. Annie just mentioned him.

ANNIE. In passing.

ELLIOT. Is he around? I'd love to meet him.

DAL. How's that?

ANNIE. Elliot, what are you doing?

ELLIOT. I just want to say hello.

ANNIE. Well, you can't. He's not here.

ELLIOT. Oh, that's a shame. Where is he?

ANNIE. He went to visit his wife.

ELLIOT. Oh, that's right. I forgot. He's married.

DAL. His wife?

ANNIE. Yes, she's in Rome on business.

DAL. I don't understand.

ANNIE. You don't understand what?

DAL. His wife died two years ago. *(Pause.)*

ANNIE. No. She's in Rome. On business.

DAL. Who told you that?

65

ANNIE.   Donald?

DAL.   Mr. Peterson?

ANNIE.   Yes.

DAL.   Donald Peterson?

ANNIE.   Yes! She's in Rome on business. He's married. Happily married. That's why … that's why … *(Annie turns away from Dal and Elliot.)*

DAL.   I'm sorry. I didn't mean to …

ELLIOT.   It's okay.

ANNIE.   *(To herself.)* He lied. He lied to me. He lied to me. *(Elliot goes to Annie. Annie stops him with a gesture.)*

DAL.   How well did you know Mr. Peterson?

ANNIE.   What? I'm sorry?

DAL.   I said, how well did you know Mr. Peterson? I don't remember seein' you at the funeral.

ANNIE.   I didn't know her. I met him after she died.

DAL.   No. His funeral. Mr. Peterson's. What was it, little over a year ago now. I don't remember seein' you. Fact, there weren't many people there at all. That cello player, the Swedish gal up on five, she was there. Played this beautiful song at the burial. Moved here after his wife passed away. He hung on for awhile and then one day Betty stopped in to check on him, y'know, see how he was doin'? And that's when she found him. With what was left of a bottle of sleepin' pills and a painting of his wife propped up in front of him. It's a beautiful picture. I got it upstairs if you wanna see it. *(Pause.)* I'm sorry if I made trouble here. I sure didn't mean to. *(Elliot walks Dal to the door.)*

ELLIOT.   No, no, it's all right.

DAL.   Is she okay?

ELLIOT.   Yeah, she'll be okay. I got her.

DAL.   I can call a doctor if you think it's necessary.

ANNIE.   Dal? *(Elliot and Dal turn back at the door.)* Is there any chance you might be thinking of a different Donald Peterson?

DAL.   I don't think so.

ANNIE.   Any chance at all?

DAL.   I'm sorry.

ANNIE.   The one who lived across the hall, right?

DAL.   He didn't live across the hall. He lived here. In 3A. This was his apartment. *(To Elliot.)* We're right upstairs if you need us.

ELLIOT.   Thanks. Appreciate it. *(Elliot and Dal disappear down the hallway.)*

DAL.   *(O.S.)* I've had a helluva time rentin' it ever since Mr. Peterson left. I'd hate to see her go. She's a good tenant.

ELLIOT.   *(O.S.)* She'll be okay. I'll make sure she's ... *(As their voices disappear, Annie stands. Slowly, unsteadily, she walks across the room. She touches the chair where Donald sat. The cellist is heard in the distance, playing the waltz. Annie turns to the D. window and listens. After a few beats, Annie quietly, slowly at first, begins to waltz. Alone. She waltzes in place, adds a half spin and then moves a little bit more until Elliot appears in the door. Elliot shuts the door behind him, almost silently. Annie is looking out.)*

ANNIE.   *(Whispering.)* Elliot? Do you ... do you know how to waltz?

ELLIOT.   What?

ANNIE.   Do you know how to waltz? Y'know. One, two, three. One, two three. One, two, three.

ELLIOT.   Yes.

ANNIE.   Liar.

ELLIOT.   No. *(Annie turns to Elliot and extends her hand.)* Oh, God. *(Elliot goes to Annie. Takes her hand. Annie places Elliot's other hand behind her back and looks up at him.)*

ANNIE.   Wish us luck. *(And slowly, quietly, they dance. The cellist continues to play the waltz. As Annie lets herself fall into Elliot's arms, the lights fade out.)*

THE END

PROPERTY LIST

Large shoulder bag (ANNIE)
Keys (DAL)
Small paint brush (DAL)
Papers (ELLIOT)
Microphone (ELLIOT)
Bag of groceries (DONALD)
Wallet containing picture of attractive woman (DONALD)
Bottle of wine, two wine glasses, bottle opener (DONALD)
Blue ice bag (DONALD, ANNIE)
Placemats, napkins, breadbasket (ANNIE)
Sketch pad (ANNIE)
Silverware (ANNIE)
Pencil (DONALD)
Menus (ANNIE, ELLIOT)
Breadstick (ELLIOT)
Woman's sweater (ELLIOT)
Large coffee table book (ELLIOT)
Piece of paper (ELLIOT)
Bag of groceries (ELLIOT)
Suitcase (ANNIE)
Twenty-dollar bill (DAL)

SOUND EFFECTS

Cello music
Siren
Phones ringing
Italian music
A waltz played on the cello

NEW PLAYS

★ **THE CREDEAUX CANVAS by Keith Bunin.** A forged painting leads to tragedy among friends. "There is that moment between adolescence and middle age when being disaffected looks attractive. Witness the enduring appeal of Prince Hamlet, Jake Barnes and James Dean, on the stage, page and screen. Or, more immediately, take a look at the lithe young things in THE CREDEAUX CANVAS..." *–NY Times.* "THE CREDEAUX CANVAS is the third recent play about painters...it turned out to be the best of the lot, better even than most plays about non-painters." *–NY Magazine.* [2M, 2W] ISBN: 0-8222-1838-0

★ **THE DIARY OF ANNE FRANK by Frances Goodrich and Albert Hackett, newly adapted by Wendy Kesselman.** A transcendently powerful new adaptation in which Anne Frank emerges from history a living, lyrical, intensely gifted young girl. "Undeniably moving. It shatters the heart. The evening never lets us forget the inhuman darkness waiting to claim its incandescently human heroine." *–NY Times.* "A sensitive, stirring and thoroughly engaging new adaptation." *–NY Newsday.* "A powerful new version that moves the audience to gasps, then tears." *–A.P.* "One of the year's ten best." *– Time Magazine.* [5M, 5W, 3 extras] ISBN: 0-8222-1718-X

★ **THE BOOK OF LIZ by David Sedaris and Amy Sedaris.** Sister Elizabeth Donderstock makes the cheese balls that support her religious community, but feeling unappreciated among the Squeamish, she decides to try her luck in the outside world. "...[a] delightfully off-key, off-color hymn to clichés we all live by, whether we know it or not." *–NY Times.* "Good-natured, goofy and frequently hilarious..." *–NY Newsday.* "...[THE BOOK OF LIZ] may well be the world's first Amish picaresque...hilarious..." *–Village Voice.* [2M, 2W (doubling, flexible casting to 8M, 7W)] ISBN: 0-8222-1827-5

★ **JAR THE FLOOR by Cheryl L. West.** A quartet of black women spanning four generations makes up this hilarious and heartwarming dramatic comedy. "...a moving and hilarious account of a black family sparring in a Chicago suburb..." *–NY Magazine.* "...heart-to-heart confrontations and surprising revelations...first-rate..." *–NY Daily News.* "...unpretentious good feelings...bubble through West's loving and humorous play..." *–Star-Ledger.* "...one of the wisest plays I've seen in ages...[from] a master playwright." *–USA Today.* [5W] ISBN: 0-8222-1809-7

★ **THIEF RIVER by Lee Blessing.** Love between two men over decades is explored in this incisive portrait of coming to terms with who you are. "Mr. Blessing unspools the plot ingeniously, skipping back and forth in time as the details require...an absorbing evening." *–NY Times.* "...wistful and sweet-spirited..." *–Variety.* [6M] ISBN: 0-8222-1839-9

★ **THE BEGINNING OF AUGUST by Tom Donaghy.** When Jackie's wife abruptly and mysteriously leaves him and their infant daughter, a pungently comic reevaluation of suburban life ensues. "Donaghy holds a cracked mirror up to the contemporary American family, anatomizing its frailties and miscommunications in fractured language that can be both funny and poignant." *–The Philadelphia Inquirer.* "...[A] sharp, eccentric new comedy. Pungently funny...fresh and precise..." *–LA Times.* [3M, 2W] ISBN: 0-8222-1786-4

★ **OUTSTANDING MEN'S MONOLOGUES 2001–2002 and OUTSTANDING WOMEN'S MONOLOGUES 2001–2002 edited by Craig Pospisil.** Drawn exclusively from Dramatists Play Service publications, these collections for actors feature over fifty monologues each and include an enormous range of voices, subject matter and characters. MEN'S ISBN: 0-8222-1821-6 WOMEN'S ISBN: 0-8222-1822-4

DRAMATISTS PLAY SERVICE, INC.
440 Park Avenue South, New York, NY 10016 212-683-8960 Fax 212-213-1539
postmaster@dramatists.com   www.dramatists.com

NEW PLAYS

★ A LESSON BEFORE DYING by Romulus Linney, based on the novel by Ernest J. Gaines. An innocent young man is condemned to death in backwoods Louisiana and must learn to die with dignity. "The story's wrenching power lies not in its outrage but in the almost inexplicable grace the characters must muster as their only resistance to being treated like lesser beings." *–The New Yorker.* "Irresistable momentum and a cathartic explosion...a powerful inevitability." *–NY Times.* [5M, 2W] ISBN: 0-8222-1785-6

★ BOOM TOWN by Jeff Daniels. A searing drama mixing small-town love, politics and the consequences of betrayal. "...a brutally honest, contemporary foray into classic themes, exploring what moves people to lie, cheat, love and dream. By BOOM TOWN's climactic end there are no secrets, only bare truth." *–Oakland Press.* "...some of the most electrifying writing Daniels has ever done..." *–Ann Arbor News.* [2M, 1W] ISBN: 0-8222-1760-0

★ INCORRUPTIBLE by Michael Hollinger. When a motley order of medieval monks learns their patron saint no longer works miracles, a larcenous, one-eyed minstrel shows them an outrageous new way to pay old debts. "A lightning-fast farce, rich in both verbal and physical humor." *–American Theatre.* "Everything fits snugly in this funny, endearing black comedy...an artful blend of the mock-formal and the anachronistically breezy...A piece of remarkably dexterous craftsmanship." *–Philadelphia Inquirer.* "A farcical romp, scintillating and irreverent." *–Philadelphia Weekly.* [5M, 3W] ISBN: 0-8222-1787-2

★ CELLINI by John Patrick Shanley. Chronicles the life of the original "Renaissance Man," Benvenuto Cellini, the sixteenth-century Italian sculptor and man-about-town. Adapted from the autobiography of Benvenuto Cellini, translated by J. Addington Symonds. "[Shanley] has created a convincing Cellini, not neglecting his dark side, and a trim, vigorous, fast-moving show." *–BackStage.* "Very entertaining...With brave purpose, the narrative undermines chronology before untangling it...touching and funny..." *–NY Times.* [7M, 2W (doubling)] ISBN: 0-8222-1808-9

★ PRAYING FOR RAIN by Robert Vaughan. Examines a burst of fatal violence and its aftermath in a suburban high school. "Thought provoking and compelling." *–Denver Post.* "Vaughan's powerful drama offers hope and possibilities." *–Theatre.com.* "[The play] doesn't put forth compact, tidy answers to the problem of youth violence. What it does offer is a compelling exploration of the forces that influence an individual's choices, and of the proverbial lifelines—be they familial, communal, religious or political—that tragically slacken when society gives in to apathy, fear and self-doubt..." *–Westword.* "...a symphony of anger..." *–Gazette Telegraph.* [4M, 3W] ISBN: 0-8222-1807-0

★ GOD'S MAN IN TEXAS by David Rambo. When a young pastor takes over one of the most prestigious Baptist churches from a rip-roaring old preacher-entrepreneur, all hell breaks loose. "...the pick of the litter of all the works at the Humana Festival..." *–Providence Journal.* "...a wealth of both drama and comedy in the struggle for power..." *–LA Times.* "...the first act is so funny...deepens in the second act into a sobering portrait of fear, hope and self-delusion..." *–Columbus Dispatch.* [3M] ISBN: 0-8222-1801-1

★ JESUS HOPPED THE 'A' TRAIN by Stephen Adly Guirgis. A probing, intense portrait of lives behind bars at Rikers Island. "...fire-breathing...whenever it appears that JESUS is settling into familiar territory, it slides right beneath expectations into another, fresher direction. It has the courage of its intellectual restlessness...[JESUS HOPPED THE 'A' TRAIN] has been written in flame." *–NY Times.* [4M, 1W] ISBN: 0-8222-1799-6

DRAMATISTS PLAY SERVICE, INC.
440 Park Avenue South, New York, NY 10016 212-683-8960 Fax 212-213-1539
postmaster@dramatists.com www.dramatists.com

NEW PLAYS

★ **THE CIDER HOUSE RULES, PARTS 1 & 2 by Peter Parnell, adapted from the novel by John Irving.** Spanning eight decades of American life, this adaptation from the Irving novel tells the story of Dr. Wilbur Larch, founder of the St. Cloud's, Maine orphanage and hospital, and of the complex father-son relationship he develops with the young orphan Homer Wells. "...luxurious digressions, confident pacing...an enterprise of scope and vigor..." *–NY Times.* "...The fact that I can't wait to see Part 2 only begins to suggest just how good it is..." *–NY Daily News.* "...engrossing...an odyssey that has only one major shortcoming: It comes to an end." *–Seattle Times.* "...outstanding...captures the humor, the humility...of Irving's 588-page novel..." *–Seattle Post-Intelligencer.* [9M, 10W, doubling, flexible casting] PART 1 ISBN: 0-8222-1725-2 PART 2 ISBN: 0-8222-1726-0

★ **TEN UNKNOWNS by Jon Robin Baitz.** An iconoclastic American painter in his seventies has his life turned upside down by an art dealer and his ex-boyfriend. "...breadth and complexity...a sweet and delicate harmony rises from the four cast members...Mr. Baitz is without peer among his contemporaries in creating dialogue that spontaneously conveys a character's social context and moral limitations..." *–NY Times.* "...darkly funny, brilliantly desperate comedy...TEN UNKNOWNS vibrates with vital voices." *–NY Post.* [3M, 1W] ISBN: 0-8222-1826-7

★ **BOOK OF DAYS by Lanford Wilson.** A small-town actress playing St. Joan struggles to expose a murder. "...[Wilson's] best work since *Fifth of July*...An intriguing, prismatic and thoroughly engrossing depiction of contemporary small-town life with a murder mystery at its core...a splendid evening of theater..." *–Variety.* "...fascinating...a densely populated, unpredictable little world." *–St. Louis Post-Dispatch.* [6M, 5W] ISBN: 0-8222-1767-8

★ **THE SYRINGA TREE by Pamela Gien.** Winner of the 2001 Obie Award. A breathtakingly beautiful tale of growing up white in apartheid South Africa. "Instantly engaging, exotic, complex, deeply shocking...a thoroughly persuasive transport to a time and a place...stun[s] with the power of a gut punch..." *–NY Times.* "Astonishing...affecting ...[with] a dramatic and heartbreaking conclusion...A deceptive sweet simplicity haunts THE SYRINGA TREE..." *–A.P.* [1W (or flexible cast)] ISBN: 0-8222-1792-9

★ **COYOTE ON A FENCE by Bruce Graham.** An emotionally riveting look at capital punishment. "The language is as precise as it is profane, provoking both troubling thought and the occasional cheerful laugh...will change you a little before it lets go of you." *–Cincinnati CityBeat.* "...excellent theater in every way..." *–Philadelphia City Paper.* [3M, 1W] ISBN: 0-8222-1738-4

★ **THE PLAY ABOUT THE BABY by Edward Albee.** Concerns a young couple who have just had a baby and the strange turn of events that transpire when they are visited by an older man and woman. "An invaluable self-portrait of sorts from one of the few genuinely great living American dramatists...rockets into that special corner of theater heaven where words shoot off like fireworks into dazzling patterns and hues." *–NY Times.* "An exhilarating, wicked...emotional terrorism." *–NY Newsday.* [2M, 2W] ISBN: 0-8222-1814-3

★ **FORCE CONTINUUM by Kia Corthron.** Tensions among black and white police officers and the neighborhoods they serve form the backdrop of this discomfiting look at life in the inner city. "The creator of this intense...new play is a singular voice among American playwrights...exceptionally eloquent..." *–NY Times.* "...a rich subject and a wise attitude." *–NY Post.* [6M, 2W, 1 boy] ISBN: 0-8222-1817-8

DRAMATISTS PLAY SERVICE, INC.
440 Park Avenue South, New York, NY 10016 212-683-8960 Fax 212-213-1539
postmaster@dramatists.com www.dramatists.com